The Wild Coast of Britain

The Wild Coast of Britain

David Bellamy

Author of *The Wild Places of Britain*

Webb & Bower

MICHAEL JOSEPH

To the memory of my father,
whose spirit is always with me
in the mountains

Also by David Bellamy:

THE WILD PLACES OF BRITAIN
PAINTING IN THE WILD

First published in Great Britain 1989 by
Webb & Bower (Publishers) Limited
5 Cathedral Close, Exeter, Devon, EX1 1EZ
in association with Michael Joseph Limited
27 Wright's Lane, London W8 5TZ

Penguin Books Ltd, Registered Offices: Harmondsworth, Middlesex,
England
Viking Penguin Inc, 40 West 23rd Street, New York, New York 10010, USA
Penguin Books Australia Ltd, Ringwood, Victoria, Australia
Penguin Books Canada Ltd, 2801 John Street, Markham, Ontario,
Canada L3R 1D4
Penguin Books (NZ) Ltd, 182–190 Wairu Road, Auckland 10, New Zealand

Designed by Peter Wrigley

Production by Nick Facer/Rob Kendrew

Text and illustrations Copyright © 1989 David Bellamy

British Library Cataloguing in Publication Data

Bellamy, David, 1943–
 The wild coast of Britain
 1. Watercolour seascape paintings. Techniques, – Manuals
 I. Title
 0–86350–292–X

Typeset in Great Britain by Keyspools Limited, Golborne, Lancashire
Colour reproduction produced by Mandarin Offset, Hong Kong
Printed and bound in Hong Kong

CONTENTS

Beachy Head

1

INTRODUCTION

Sailing Dinghy, Porlock Weir

Kittiwakes wheeled in tight circles, their strident cries echoing hauntingly above a moving sculpture of foaming surf as it splashed onto the sea-carved rock of Flimston Bay in Pembrokeshire. The birds, as they swirled and soared to the song of the waves, epitomized the freedom and beauty of this wild but ecologically fragile coast where man, the intruder, is sometimes slow to grasp one of his most precious assets. When I set out to celebrate this glorious coastline in words and pictures, it was something of a voyage into uncharted territory. Not so much the actual coast, but the whole approach: exploring new areas, going out to sea, meeting all sorts of people connected with the sea, and trying to marry up the results in notes and sketches. I am not a seafaring person, hardly knowing the difference between a Loch Fyne double-ender and an Old Gaffer, and much of it was totally new to me. So what is a mountain artist doing writing a book on the coast? Although my marine paintings are not as well known as my mountain work, I do a considerable number, mainly based on scenes in my native Pembrokeshire. I cannot stress strongly enough what a tremendous influence and inspiration the county has had on my work. Having been brought up there, with the sea on three sides, it is difficult not to be influenced by such a stunning coastline. I well remember the most commonly sung hymn in morning assembly at Narberth Grammar School was William Whiting's masterpiece 'Eternal Father, strong to save', that ended:

O hear us when we cry to thee,
For those in peril on the sea.

Additionally, when I spent a few years in London, I fell under the spell of the Suffolk coast, and though very different from the Pembrokeshire coast, I did some interesting work there. Then, one day, whilst on a visit to Exmoor, I decided to explore part of the North Devon coast. It left such a profound impression on my imagination that I felt the strong urge to write a book celebrating the wilder parts of the coastline. The coast has much in common with mountains – bare rock, exposure to the elements, and rough going in places, plus a certain

romance that is hard to define. When nature is angry it evokes a savage picture on coast or mountain.

Although I was born within hailing distance of the sea, at Pembroke, I grew up with little interest in it. Except, that is, for a burning ambition, not to become an engine-driver when I grew up, but to be a pirate. A nice pirate of course! Perhaps I was influenced by Pembrokeshire's most famous pirate, Bartholomew Roberts, or Black Barty as he is better known. Barty was probably the most successful and colourful character to sail under the skull and crossbones, the flag which he invented and which was later copied by other pirates the world over. Kidd and Morgan, both better known pirates, pale into insignificance beside this Preseli lad. Starting his career during

Port Isaac
This narrow alleyway leading up from the harbour provided an interesting subject. There are many such in Port Isaac, with at least one where I had to turn sideways to squeeze through.

Sunrise, River Helford
The original sketch was done on the yacht *Caenswood*, moored in mid channel. After a glorious sunset it was quite something waking up to this scene at the opposite end of the river.

the War of the Spanish Succession at the beginning of the eighteenth century, he then worked on a slave ship out of the Gold Coast until it was taken as a prize by the pirate Hywel Davies from Milford Haven. Davies persuaded Barty to join him on the *Royal Rover*, one of the fastest ships afloat. Shortly afterwards, Davies was killed in action and Barty was elected captain. In one of his first actions as captain, Barty sailed the *Royal Rover* into a fleet of forty-two well armed Portuguese men-o'-war off Brazil. Though outgunned forty to one he made off with a prize ship, the *Sagrada Familia*, brimming with gold, skins, sugar and tobacco, for the loss of two men, an event unparalleled in the history of piracy. Barty forbade gambling and women on board and no prizes were to be taken on Sundays. Before engaging in battle he would appear on deck dressed all over in crimson, with a large red feather in his hat, whilst a band played on the poop deck. His reputation spread before him. The French called him *le Joli Rouge*, which later turned into the name for the pirate flag, the Jolly Roger. An entire French fleet anchored off Newfoundland then submitted to his ransacking under the stare of forty French cannon and 1200 soldiers. To the accompaniment of music, of course! He virtually cleared shipping from the seas in the West Indies, then decided to have more fun off Africa. Here the Governors of the Royal African Company sent out a frigate but this was rapidly despatched by the pirate. Eventually, in 1722, Barty was cornered by two British men-o'-war when his crew were heavily drunk. The first broadside killed Barty and eventually the pirates surrendered.

That sort of tale is bound to stir the blood of any young lad,

Mew Stone, Skomer Island
From Skomer itself the dramatic impact of this crag is not really apparent, but from Jack Sound it stands out strongly, all the more impressive when teeming with sea birds. This painting was done on Canson paper using Derwent soft pastels.

Rock arch near Solva
I first caught sight of this arch from the cliff top, at a hopeless angle for sketching, so I decided to try sketching from a boat. The low angle adds to the powerful impression. From a boat much more wildlife is visible, and I recommend artists to try it, but preferably in calm weather and with someone else to pilot the boat, especially on a wild coast like Pembrokeshire. I was lucky to have

Paul Hemming valiantly keeping the boat on station at just the right point, and making sure we didn't hit anything. Paul runs the Twr-y-Felin outdoor centre with his mate Andy Middleton, and if you want an exciting day on the Pembrokeshire coast I recommend them highly. The final painting has been painted in oils on board.
From the collection of the author

but when we went down to Tenby one day I took one look at the sea and decided that piracy wasn't such a good idea. The sea looked distinctly rough. One of my earliest memories of drama at sea was the electrifying broadcasts on the radio during the thirteen-day epic of the *Flying Enterprise* in January 1952. The crippled ship was being towed by the tug *Turmoil*. The world held its breath as the ship, listing by sixty degrees with only her skipper, Captain Carlsen, and Ken Dancy, a tug-man, on board, was slowly being towed towards Falmouth. Sadly she sank with some sixty miles still to go. Some of these accounts of man's battles with stormy seas are related in the fol-lowing pages. I find it impossible not to be moved by many of the tragedies associated with the sea, for those whose living depends on it are constantly at risk. Even these days, no hi-tech advance will ever conquer its fearsome might. Once the weather turns nasty any craft losing power will be fortunate not to be pounded to pieces on the rocky anvils of the coast. There are times when almost whole villages have been affected by the severity of the sea, such as the great gale of 1881 when Eye-mouth, north of Berwick-on-Tweed, lost 129 fishermen within sight of their loved ones.

Although I was familiar with much of the British coastline, I

felt that in order to write a book about it, I would need to experience what it was like to be out at sea in a small boat. My first experience in charge of a boat, many years ago, was pretty disastrous; I went into a lock on the Thames rather too fast, couldn't find the 'brake', and only just managed to slow the cabin cruiser down before coming to a gentle, undignified bump against the far lock-gate, much to the lock-keeper's disgust. I felt somewhat like Toad of Toad Hall, but soon, unlike Toad, got the hang of it all. So, in a small way I have taken to the sea, albeit warily, for, as the Irish writer J M Synge, in a short prose on the Aran Islands off the west coat of Ireland, wrote, 'A man who is not afraid of the sea will soon be drownded, he said, for he will be going out on a day he shouldn't. But we do be afraid of the sea, and we do only be drownded now and again.'

I would like to write about a beautiful coast, unadulterated by the effluence of modern Britain, but sadly those in authority do not seem to care much for the state of our environment. I've sat on rocks to sketch and come away with tar and oil on my trousers; I've swum in the sea in places, only to return home sick for several days; I can no longer let my daughter Catherine build sandcastles on certain beaches because of dog excrement; some harbours look like burst sewers; on one visit to the coast I returned to the car to find a used nappy beside it; we don't seem to care what we dump in the sea, even if it is highly toxic or radioactive. Every ship adds to the filth and some of our rivers run almost red in places with pollution from industry and agriculture. Fish are being contaminated and seals are dying. I shall not dwell on these aspects, but feel very strongly about the manner in which we are destroying such beauty.

This book is organized into eleven chapters covering parts of the coast from Scotland to Dorset, followed by a chapter dem-onstrating my methods of sketching and painting, plus a chapter devoted to practical aspects of walking on the coast. There is no way that one book could cover the whole of the British coast, not even just the wild places. Nor would I wish to do so, as it would then be impossible to cover any area in reasonable depth. So, of necessity, it has to be a selective and very personal collection. What constitutes a wild section is open to debate, but what follows is my choice, although sadly, many wild parts have had to be omitted because of lack of space.

It has been an extremely enjoyable experience working on this book, and in many ways I feel sad that it had to end. What has impressed me enormously is the response and kindnesses of the seafaring folk. The lifeboatmen, the fishermen, the coastguards, the helicopter rescue crews, the boat-builders, and many more associated with the sea have been generous with their time and patience for an ignorant landlubber. I only hope this book will do justice to these kind and brave people. I owe them a great debt.

Roll on, thou deep and dark blue ocean – roll!
Ten thousand fleets sweep over thee in vain;
Man marks the earth with ruin – his control
Stops with the shore; – upon the watery plain
The wrecks are all thy deed, nor doth remain
A shadow of man's ravage, save his own,
When, for a moment, like a drop of rain,
He sinks into thy depths with bubbling groan,
Without a grave, unknelled, uncoffined, and unknown

Lord Byron, 'Childe Harold's Pilgrimage'

LEFT
Wild waves
A watercolour sketch done at the edge of the rocks on a wild day east of Manorbier Bay. Unfortunately the sketch became creased in the howling wind, but the fierce drizzle has added to the atmosphere by spotting the dark washes. Visibility was extremely poor, but this is not necessarily a bad thing for the artist. Detail has been added with a black watercolour pencil.

OVERLEAF
***Lord* Approaching Kinvara**
In lowering skies, with Dún Guaire Castle in the background, the *leath bhád Lord* is seen returning to Kinvara harbour. *Leath bhád*, pronounced 'La Wawd', means a half-boat, and is similar to a Galway Hooker, only smaller.

2
SALT-WATER LOCHS

Altandhu
This cottage is one of several
straggling around the hamlet of
Altandhu on this bleak but stunning
part of the coast of Wester Ross.

The western seaboard of the Scottish Highlands, from the Isle of Arran to Cape Wrath, is a wild, confusing coastline where, in places, though still on the mainland, one seems to be surrounded by water, unable to define what is a sea-loch, or what is a strait. In places the mountains tumble fjord-like right down to sea-level in spectacular drops. There are few places of refuge from the savage storms that rend these shores. One only has to climb to the summit of Suilven, which towers almost sheer above the barren moorlands of Assynt, and gaze seawards to get an idea of the nature of this inhospitable coastline. The gleaming silvery sea lies beyond a grotesquely contorted shoreline, and nearer to hand lie myriads of sparkling lochans, too numerous to count. One wild September day I stood on Caisteal Liath, the higher of Suilven's twin summits and witnessed a storm coming in from the south west. With amazing suddenness massive thunderclouds built up. In a trice the sparkle was doused, replaced by a violent darkness: a graphic example of how rapidly a boat at sea can be caught out in alarming conditions. I was thankful to be on the mountain, on terra firma, although the wind threatened to tear me off the narrow ridge as I began the descent. Nearly all afternoon I could see storms approach and fade away, but none reached Suilven.

These western shores have seen the coming of the saints from Ireland: St Brendan, that great seafarer, St Columba, who in 563 founded the Celtic church on the isle of Iona, and of course many others. Then came the sudden, savage incursions by the Norsemen, who dominated the coastal areas in their fast longships for some four centuries, looting, pillaging and generally running amok without any effective opposition. For many years the Western Isles came under the rule of King Magnus of Norway – in 1098 for the sake of peace they were ceded to Norway when the Norsemen threatened to spread further inland. The agreement was that Magnus could have power over every island, an island being defined as being completely circumnavigable by a fully equipped longship. Magnus must have been a wily old joker, however, as he grabbed the peninsula of the Mull of Kintyre by dragging a longship across the isthmus. The Norsemen were finally beaten in 1263 at the

Sandwood Bay and Am Buachaille
Sandwood Bay has a beautiful, sandy beach, devoid of people, being so remote. A great pillar of rock rears dramatically out of the sea near the cliffs. This is Am Buachaille, the Shepherd.

Suilven from Lochinver
When I first looked out of the window only the harbour was visible. Then as the mist slowly cleared the amazing shape of Suilven was revealed, towering over the little port. It really is one of the most remarkably shaped mountains in the Highlands.

David Bellamy

LEFT
Scottish Puffer
When I first saw this vessel I couldn't believe my eyes – the amount of smoke coming out of the funnel was incredible. No wonder they called these boats 'puffers'. Puffers have been carrying coastal cargoes around Scotland for many years, but there are not many about now.

ABOVE
Plockton
Plockton is an artist's dream, with whitewashed houses sitting singly or in rows, according to your taste. Add in the boats and mountains and you have all the ingredients for a painting.

Loch Broom

Battle of Largs, on the firth of Clyde, by a Scots army under Alexander III, with considerable help from the weather.

It was the wild nature of the sea-lochs that helped Bonnie Prince Charlie to elude the attentions of English frigates when he departed from Loch nan Uamh in 1746 on board the French frigate *L'Heureux*. These west highland lochs make superb painting subjects, even on days of foul weather, for the lighting is often dramatic and the lochs themselves form interesting compositions. Knoydart, scene of many of the prince's adventures, is a sparsely populated area, where many old crofts stand deserted by shore and on hillsides, roofless, forlorn and open to the elements, some barely more than a pile of stones. The sea-lochs appear to be sheltered, but can in fact be extremely rough when strong winds are funnelled in between high and steep mountainsides that descend to the water's edge. This was brought home to me when riding in a dory on Upper Loch

Hourn one boisterous September morning. Heading for Kinloch Hourn we encountered extremely powerful head winds coming straight down the loch. The craft stuttered its way along the five miles or so, constantly being hit by waves which crashed over the bows and drenched us in the open boat. Sailing these waters in reasonable weather, however, gives a new perspective to this spectacular landscape. A boat certainly provides tremendous flexibility when planning to climb a mountain in the Western Highlands, and can eliminate a considerable amount of walking to reach the foot of a mountain.

Further up the coast on the shore of Loch Carron is the picturesque little village of Plockton, much loved by artist and tourist alike. Around the corner, at Loch Kishorn, in the shadow of the impressive peaks of the Applecross Forest, are oil-rigs. These massive eyesores rise up like giant unmade bedsteads, and look totally out of place amongst such great natural

Bay of Culkein
The distant headland was extremely dark in the strange lighting when I did this watercolour sketch on the spot. Normally when painting a landscape the darkest tones are retained in the foreground to give an illusion of depth, but there are always exceptions to the rule.

Firth of Clyde

I thought that the frigate was going to hit our stern as it charged towards us, but it did enable me to get a close-up picture. In this final painting I have used pastels, mainly to achieve the soft blending of the distant hills. At the time I was crossing by ferry to the Isle of Arran.

Castle Stalker

beauty. Man has been responsible for some strange developments in many of these lochs: apart from oil-rigs, a torpedo testing station was established at Loch Long, and many lochs are now being visually defaced by an escalating number of fish farms. Whilst these bring much needed employment to areas that offer little alternatives for work, development should be more stringently controlled before the situation gets out of hand and some of the truly beautiful lochs are spoilt.

At Ullapool the ferries and trawlers ply to and fro, whilst the large factory ships seem to just sit there. These latter vessels bristle with derricks, their hulls showing rust-slicks, grey ships against a background of grey mountains and grey seas, punctuated at times with a silver strand of light. These days the town seems full of eastern bloc fishermen who come ashore in ships' orange lifeboats: tin cans with a keel and propellor. Scottish fishing vessels sell their fish to these factory ships, which are not allowed to fish British waters. One night I watched the twinkling lights of the trawlers from the edge of Scourie Bay, as the vessels moved back and forth across the bay in unison. In the early days of trawling with one hundred or more vessels fishing together at night collisions often occurred and many smaller boats were run down and sunk. Once the men were washed overboard there was little that could save them in their heavy clothing. Fishing is still listed officially as the most dangerous occupation in the British Isles. Before the twentieth century it must have been even more so, with the appalling conditions that prevailed. Compared to the east coast of Scotland the western side is a cauldron of violent and dangerous waters, with few safe harbours to run to in a storm. As a consequence the full-time fishing industry on the west coast worked at a considerable disadvantage when compared with other parts of the country. Today's fishermen, despite modern comforts and electronic aids that can detect a single cod at 1500 feet, still have to work on an exposed deck sorting out the catch in all weather conditions.

Not far above Scourie, on the northern shore of Loch Inchard, lies the fishing village of Kinlochbervie. One night, whilst out for a stroll, I was amazed to find the harbour a hive of industry. Many large modern fishing vessels were tied up

and work was progressing, at what seemed breakneck speed, on a large new building. Here, the fish would be unloaded for further transport in refrigerated fish trucks. It all seemed so incongruous in such a small remote community. Kinlochbervie has a number of attractive dwellings to sketch, and a little further along the coast road at Oldshoremore and Blairmore the mixture of cottages, cliffs and coastline is an artist's dream. My visit to Oldshoremore coincided with a storm coming in from the sea, so it was something of a treat to sit in the comparative comfort of the car there during the storm. Although the car received quite a buffeting I came away with some interesting work.

From Blairmore a rough track leads northwards to Sandwood Bay, a favourite walk for those who love wild, remote beaches. But you won't see many people there. From the sandy beach views stretch northwards towards Cape Wrath. The cliffs around Cape Wrath are sites for great colonies of puffins, guillemots, razorbills and fulmars, though the sea eagles have long gone from this spot. Rising out of the sea at the western extremity of the bay is the eye-rivetting sandstone pinnacle of Am Buachaille, the Shepherd. Just inland lies Sandwood Loch. Unfortunately its lovely western shore attracts many campers who don't seem to care too much about leaving litter – it's everywhere, and if that wasn't enough some miscreants had even dragged bits of flotsam up from the seashore. Above the loch Sandwood House is a mere shell, but on that day smoke rose from its chimney. Someone must have been using it as a bothy . . . or had the ghost returned?

A few days after exploring Sandwood Bay my travels brought me to the shores of Loch Eriboll on the north coast. The loch is a fine place for artists. Apart from a distant view of Ben Hope it is not endowed with the dramatic scenery of many of the western lochs, but there are a number of beautifully sited cottages along its western shore. These make superb subjects with the loch as a backdrop. Surprisingly, the loch is around 350 feet (107 metres) deep in places which made it useful during World War II for assembling North Atlantic convoys. I was actually driving round to Strath Beag, but it took me all afternoon as I kept stopping to sketch every few yards. That, however, was the end of any comfortable sketching for one day. Once into Strath Beag where the main objective was to check out a bothy for possible use by the Mountain Bothies Association, I quickly became extremely wet fording streams, very sore with briars tearing at me, and when I did stop to sketch I was almost eaten alive by midges. Although I've had many a pitched battle with midgies I've yet to find an effective deterrent. A friend in Inverness advised using perfume to repel them, but I've not yet had the courage to try that one out!

The glens running inland from the north coast of Scotland are peppered with the remains of old buildings, and were once heavily populated before the Clearances of the eighteenth and nineteenth centuries devastated the land. After the Battle of Culloden in 1746 the old clan system was abolished and the clan chiefs became lairds, owners of land that formerly belonged to the whole clan. Following the example of the south-ern gentry the new lairds were eager to make their estates highly profitable, and so introduced sheep to the highlands. Families were evicted, their homes, crops and belongings set on fire without giving the terrified victims time even to salvage any of their possessions. The manner in which it was all carried out was totally inhumane, the people being treated worse than animals. The government in Westminster took no notice of their plight. Desperately they turned to the coast. Some lived in caves, crude shelters, hovels or whatever they could manage, and tried to scrape a living from the barren wind-torn coast in abject poverty. But they still had to pay rent to their landlords, and in many areas even had to pay for the seaweed they collected to burn over peat fires to produce a fertilizer. For many there was nothing for it but to emigrate. To be forced to leave a homeland as beautiful as this, never to return, must have been absolutely heartbreaking.

Rain clearing, Loch Ailort
Pastels are excellent for suggesting a veil of rain or snow falling across distant mountains. This is fine walking terrain, if you can stand the wetness! It does happen to be one of the wettest places in the country.

3
COBLES, CASTLES AND KIPPERS

ABOVE
Robin Hood's Bay

LEFT
Fishing coble
A painting done on De Wint tinted paper which has an extremely rough surface. The low key approach helps to convey the atmosphere of loneliness of a small boat amidst a wide sea and intimidating cliffs.

Creeping about in the half-light of dawn seems an unholy and definitely furtive habit. Whilst in the high mountains there is hardly ever anyone around to witness such antics, in a town or village you never know who is watching and wondering why you are lurking in an alleyway. When you are an artist out sketching some people conjure up all sorts of ideas as to what you may be doing.

Whilst most of England slept I had crawled out of my tent and descended into Robin Hood's Bay from the misty rolling North York Moors. The upper houses cut strong lines against a background of light sea mist. Though eager to get down to shore level, I sketched rapidly, not wanting to miss a subject so full of atmosphere. There always seems to be a frenetic urgency first thing in the morning when I need to capture so much on paper before things can be seen too clearly. It is not necessarily a good thing to be able to see in detail what you are painting, as light mist automatically simplifies the scene, induces an air of mystery, and leaves much to the imagination.

Robin Hood's Bay was a great place for smugglers in bygone days, when many of the local community became involved in the trade. The village is said to be riddled with tunnels and secret hideaways. Less welcome were the visits by His Majesty's press-gangs, though apparently the local lads took some catching whilst their womenfolk confronted the gangs with Amazonian ferocity. But why was it called Robin Hood's Bay? Some tales say Robin came here to flee to Europe, whilst others reckoned that he came to help repel Danish invaders. Whilst here he was not averse to robbing the abbot's servants, but it must be said to his credit that it appears that 'he showed his favour to the local harrassed farmers'!

Descending the narrow streets in the pale winter light I soon reached the sea-front, where houses virtually tumble into the North Sea. Very little stirred as I walked along the seashore. A gentle sunlight shimmered through the mist, catching the crest of each wave as it broke. Sketching is a delight early in the morning when the light is often at its best. Also there are fewer people around – it can be distracting to an artist to be constantly bombarded with questions. The mist simplified the composition and after sketching the bay I turned my attention to the village, finding a comfortable seat on a boat. Amazingly there seemed to be a gull perched on every chimney-pot. At first things were fine and the watercolour sketch progressed well, until suddenly an over-friendly dog appeared. With its tail wagging furiously it tried to lick my face. Still sitting down, I shied away, moving the rucksack in between us, and held the sketch high in the air. I resumed sketching. The dog, frustrated by the rucksack, turned its attention to the sketch and began to lick my nicely laid wet wash. This in no way improved the work, and so when the animal refused to oblige to 'please go away', I raised both my legs in the air and held the sketchbook closer to my body. Fido wasn't having any of this, however, and with one great leap shot over the rucksack and landed on top of sketchbook and artist. With a clatter of painting equipment we rolled over into the boat, accompanied by several large smelly lobster pots and the rucksack. Unfortunately, by now I had an audience: maybe they get regular entertainment by artists in Robin Hood's Bay?

By contrast my visit to Whitby, just to the north of Robin Hood's Bay, was less hazardous and I was able to mix with the large crowds and sketch almost unnoticed. The art of sketching on quays in these conditions is to position yourself so that no one can look over your shoulder whilst you are working: this can be achieved by standing on the very edge of the quay, but of course you have to be aware at all times of exactly where you are standing! Whitby, where Captain Cook learned to sail, has inspired many great artists and it is easy to see why. The abbey ruins, perched high above the town, form a picturesque backdrop to the bustling harbour. There are some fine atmospheric watercolours of old Whitby by George Weatherill(1810–90), a native of Staithes, in the Pannett Art Gallery in the town, and of course John Atkinson Grimshaw (1836–93) painted many scenes here on the waterfront. He was particularly well known for his moonlit harbour and romantic twilight scenes, lit by the hazy glow of gas lamps reflected in the still waters of the harbour. One of the more modern artists to interest me was Robert Howey, who painted local scenes with particular emphasis on Whitby and Runswick Bay. His highly individual use of opaque pigments in heavy impasto with watercolours on tinted papers intrigued me, with their atmospheric effects and use of a limited palette. Most of his paintings depicted coastal scenes in which the coble featured largely.

Modern cobles swung at their moorings in the harbour as I sketched. They are fascinating boats, quite different in design from any other in the country. Cobles are clinker-built with flat bottoms and high bows. The strong distinguishing features of these traditional fishing boats are long tillers and raked flat sterns which help the waves to carry them off or push them up onto the shore. In bad weather they can be beached stern first. These days they are normally used for line and pot fishing, and powered by a petrol or diesel engine. In bygone days they carried a large rectangular dipping lugsail and were mainly employed in catching herring.

The cobles drawn up in tight ranks at Staithes a few miles to the north of Whitby were some of the most gaily painted craft I have seen in Britain, the colour perhaps more in keeping with Mediterranean vessels. Staithes must be one of the most painted places in North Yorkshire. Nestling under high cliffs, it contains many inviting nooks and crannies. Much erosion is taking place along this coast, and at Staithes the Cod and Lobster Inn has been washed away three times, and was last rebuilt in 1953. My first reaction was to back excitedly into the middle of the stream that runs down into the harbour, where there was a fine view of cobles and houses. Perched on two reasonably large stones I then began work.

'You a real artist, mister?' The question sprang from a young lad standing nearby. I detected a slight ring of puzzlement. Perhaps real artists are not expected to stand in the middle of streams. Or maybe it was the hat that put him off. Little boys

Robin Hood's Bay
Early morning sunlight catches the ends of the houses which stop just short of the sea.

Staithes
Staithes is a fishing village much loved by artists and photographers. The gaily painted cobles crammed into the narrow stream liven up the scene. The white flecks on the red cliffs are masses of seagulls.

David Bellamy

Lindisfarne (watercolour)
In this final painting I have tried to retain the simplicity of the original sketch (overleaf). It is all too easy to begin painting in extra detail, real or imaginary. At times artists use their brain too much when painting, at the expense of the visual messages coming from the subject. An example of this would be where detailed stonework is included when from the viewing distance of the artist individual stones could not actually be picked out.

are never easy to shake off, and this one stuck like chewing gum on a fairy's wand. We ended up doing several sketches together.

The coast further north in Northumberland brought quite a contrast. Gone were the red cliffs and crowds, and here was an equally beautiful coast, a coast of castles – Dunstanburgh, Bamburgh, and Lindisfarne, or Holy Island. The sea was rather lively as we walked up the coast from Craster, famous for its kipper-curing. It is only about a mile to Dunstanburgh Castle, now a ruin. Built in the fourteenth century on a rocky promontory, it has remained unaltered throughout its history. I stopped to sketch the gaunt ruin from some flat rocks and became so involved in the painting that I didn't notice that the tide was coming in. With remarkable suddenness a massive wave crashed over the rock, liberally wetting both sketch and artist. I retreated quickly and completed the sketch from a drier position.

Normally I tend not to like hot sunny days for sketching, but the hot sunshine at Lindisfarne was tempered by interesting and massive cloud formations. Of the whole east coast of Britain, surely this is the most romantic castle? Formerly a ruined sixteenth-century fort it was recreated in 1902 by Sir Edwin Lutyens. When the tide comes in it completely covers the causeway, effectively cutting the island off from the mainland. The monastery was founded by St Aidan in 635, and from here he began the conversion of Saxon England. It was destroyed by the Danes in the ninth century. In 1093 building began on a priory, the ruins of which still stand today. The castle makes a superb composition from many angles, but for my first sketch I sat beside some enormous black hulks, the remnants of the old herring fleet, now used as huts. They were cut in half and turned upside down, then arranged along the shore like a row of stunted and stranded whales.

Further out to sea are the Farne Islands, and in 1838 it was from Farne Island itself that Grace Darling and her father, keeper of the Longstone lighthouse, rowed a coble nearly half a mile across a turbulent sea to the steamer *Forfarshire* which had struck Big Harcar rock. They took nine survivors off the rock, including one woman holding the bodies of her two dead children in her arms. Their coble was not a lifeboat, however. The first purpose-built lifeboat is generally accepted to have been a Northumbrian idea. It came about in 1789 when a prize

Lindisfarne (sketch)

was offered by a club in North Shields for the design of a life-boat. This was inspired by the loss of the ship *Adventure* with all its crew off South Shields. The resulting boat was thirty feet (9.15 metres) long, carried six pairs of oars and was built on the self-righting principle, with a lot of cork being used in the construction. It served the community for about forty years.

This is a truly special coast, to a large extent greatly unspoilt. Sadly, however, out at sea things are far from being rosy. The North Sea is becoming Britain's dustbin, with incineration at sea of hazardous wastes and much dumping. The Tees and Humber are two of our most heavily polluted rivers, and as a consequence we are seeing much of the wildlife being devastated: seals are dying in their thousands. Even the coast itself is not free from pollution, with colliery waste being dumped on the beaches of Durham. How much longer must it go on before we are overwhelmed by a mass of filth and disease? Paradoxically it may well be one of the most beautiful parts of the east coast which bears the brunt of this deplorable state of affairs.

They toss their sad, spent jetsam in the sea –
cheap artefacts our throw-away society
scatters, ocean-wide; each man consigns
his message in disposable designs.

Jean M Thomas

Bamburgh Castle
The castle stands on a rock plinth some 150 feet (46 metres) above the sea. A fortification was first built by the early kings of Northumbria but, true to form, was later ransacked by the Danes.

Yr Eifl
When seen from this position at Porth Dinllaen, the almost vertical drop of the hills into the sea looks awesome. Sailing dinghies suggested a sense of scale, but even so, these are only hills when compared to the giants of Snowdonia not far away.

4
FROM DRUIDS TO
DWYRYD PHILISTINES

Abersoch

Abersoch is a lovely old place, the centre of the yachting establishment on the Lleyn. This is an original watercolour sketch, showing mess-marks caused by the scramble when a deluge arrived just as I had finished. Rarely does the weather allow me such privileges!

The coast of North Wales is perhaps neglected by many because of the close proximity of the glorious delights of the Snowdonia National Park, but nevertheless it is a coast blessed with superb and varied scenery. Major attractions on this coast are the great castles of Conwy, Caernarfon, Beaumaris and Harlech. Conwy has always been one of my favourites as a subject, with the great turretted battlements standing as an impressive backdrop to boats tied up at the quay. The castle was completed in 1292 as part of Edward I's chain of coastal castles designed to be provisioned from the sea. In 1401 it was overrun by the Welsh one Sunday whilst the garrison attended evensong. Unfortunately, from many angles, the view of the castle has been spoilt by the ugly modern road and railway bridges.

After one visit to Conwy I moved on to Anglesey, Ynys Môn, where in AD 61 those demonic Druids and their wild naked women ranged up in demented hordes against the invading Roman armies. My first visit to the island brought new problems from a working point of view, as my friend and guide appeared to be in constant need of frequent liquid refreshment. Hence, many of my earliest scenes of Anglesey originated in the gardens of pubs – not the best of vantage points on a freezing winter morning! I remember vividly the biting wind as I sketched in Cemaes Bay, not helped by the liquid intake, although some unkind comments suggested afterwards a definite improvement in my technique. . . . Nearby at Amlwch the harbour was blasted out of solid rock to ship out the copper from the Parys Mountain Copper Mine. The miners worked in appalling conditions of near slavery, and yet it became a sort of tourist attraction, on the tour of many artists, including Sandby and Ibbetson.

The Anglesey coast, being on the main shipping route to Liverpool from the south, has seen many great sea tragedies. At Moelfre the Lifeboat Station has been involved in many epic rescues over the years. One such epic occurred on 27 October 1959, when at lunchtime the station received a frantic message from the coastguard to say that a vessel was dragging her anchor and about to be blown onto rocks in Lligwy Bay, a mere half mile from the lifeboat slipway. The *Edmund and Mary Robinson* slid down the slipway into the wildest seas imaginable, with winds gusting at over 100 mph. Unable to contact many of the crew, Coxswain Richard Evans had only four in his crew, and one a novice who had never before been in a lifeboat. It took one and a half hours to cover the half mile to the 500-ton *MV Hindlea* which was yawing violently on her anchor chain. Massive waves were breaking over the ship, with eight men clinging to her rails as the lifeboat made her run in on the port quarter. Then the great stern of the *Hindlea* rose out of the sea, the massive propellors clawing thin air just feet above the tiny lifeboat, which would have been cut to ribbons had they made contact. As she came up out of the trough the lifeboat was caught by an immense wave, knocking her over and capsizing her. How the hearts of those eight men on the ship must have sunk as the lifeboat disappeared. Moments later she rose out of the water, unbowed, as game as ever. She crashed against the *Hindlea* and the first man jumped aboard to safety. In moments the lifeboat was washed away from the ship. It needed several more runs to get off the remaining survivors, but as the lifeboat approached the vessel for the last time she was lifted up the side of the ship and dumped unceremoniously on the deck of the *Hindlea*. Just as the last man was hauled aboard another wave lifted the lifeboat clear, but desperately close to the rocks. It needed some skilled manoeuvring to get her back to Moelfre. Coxswain Evans was awarded the highest honour that can be won by a lifeboatman, an RNLI gold medal. Seven years later he was awarded a second, something that is very rare indeed. For this rescue mechanic Evan Owen received a silver medal, and the other three in the crew bronze medals.

The west coast of Anglesey is riven with rocky bays, best seen when a fiery sunset lights the sky out to sea. One February I encountered a glorious sunset every night I was on the island. In contrast to these rocky shores is Newborough Warren in the south west of the island. Here is the largest area of sand dunes on the west coast of Britain. In the fourteenth century the area was associated with Dafydd ap Gwilym, the greatest of all Welsh poets. Nearby, on the Cefni estuary lies the village of Malltraeth where the bird artist Charles Tunnicliffe lived from 1947 to 1979, the year he died. During that period he rarely left

Anglesey. He lived by the shore in a house with spectacular views of the mountains of Snowdonia. Malltraeth Pool provided a source of great inspiration for him, for it is noted for its waders: curlew, greenshanks, redshanks, sandpipers and lapwings, which use the estuary as a migratory staging-post.

Just south west of Anglesey at Dinas Dinlle there is a stunning view of Yr Eifl, better known as The Rivals to English visitors. The view is even more dramatic from the west at Porth Dinllaen, where the mountains drop down almost vertically to the surf below at Trwyn y Gorlech. It is hard to realise that they are only 1850 feet (564 metres) high. I visited Porth Dinllaen with my daughter Catherine one beautiful October day, and whilst she collected some attractive whelk shells and built sandcastles, I sketched. In earlier times Porth Dinllaen was a bustling port and built its own ships. It was even considered at one time as a potential ferry port for Ireland.

At the tip of the Lleyn Peninsula, a sort of Welsh Land's End without the commercial trappings, stands Mynydd Mawr, a strange name for a hill only 524 feet (159 metres) high. The summit commands a magnificent view of Bardsey Island, 'The Isle of Saints', about two and a half miles across the fast flowing waters of Bardsey Sound. Nearby Abersoch is quite a contrast to the rest of the Lleyn: it is the playground of the yachting fraternity, with a few working boats for good measure. One of the fishing boats had been superbly positioned with an interesting background. A comfortable seat was even provided in the form of a boat trailer, so in hot sunshine I began sketching, wondering what I'd done to deserve all this. Suddenly, Catherine decided to bounce up and down on the far end of the trailer, bringing my sky-high thoughts down to earth with quite a bump. In winter the local community changes markedly, for in places here up to half the dwellings are second homes.

Where the River Glaslyn meets the sea after flowing down from the heart of the great mountains of Snowdonia, lies Porthmadog. According to legend it was from here that Prince Madog sailed to discover America even before Columbus. Formerly a ship-building port which exported slates, it is now used by the leisure boaters. Slate was brought down from the Ffestiniog quarries by packhorse in the early days, transferring to horse and cart above Maentwrog. It was then brought to Gelligrin wharf where it was loaded onto barges by a group of strangely clad boatmen called Philistines. Heavily tanned, their striking appearance was further enhanced by knee-breeches and large black felt hats which made them look extremely tall. The slate was then taken by barge down the River Dwyryd to Ynys Cyngar to be loaded onto the ships. In 1824 work started on building Porthmadog harbour and a year later ships were being loaded there. In 1833 a railway was proposed, but the Philistines and their supporters opposed it in Parliament. In 1834 the railway company tried again and was successful, and two years later the Ffestiniog Railway was born. At first a gravity system operated, whereby the slate-filled wagons would roll down the gentle gradient, two of the wagons carrying horses to pull the empty wagons back to Blaenau Ffestiniog. Until the outbreak of World War I Porthmadog had strong trading links with Hamburg.

The port was also famous for its wooden ships, made from materials almost entirely of local origin. Porthmadog schooners were the ultimate development of the small wooden merchant sailing ship in the British Isles, being superior in structure and materials to any of their contemporaries. Everywhere they went, their graceful lines were admired, and envied by ship designers. Locally there was a great need for sturdy seaworthy vessels, for the approach to Porthmadog was difficult with a shifting channel and treacherous coastline. Sarn Badrig (St Patrick's Causeway) extends some twenty miles out to sea from a tongue of land west of Llanbedr. St Patrick is said to have used it to cross to Ireland. Part of it can be seen at low water and it has claimed many vessels. The Porthmadog topsail schooners had just the right rig for beating clear from Sarn Badrig. These rigs were introduced by the Porthmadog ship designers to cope with both the problems of navigating in these restricted waters and for deep-sea sailing. The schooners from this little port not only visited the Mediterranean, but also sailed the Atlantic with cargoes of salt-cod from Newfoundland and to fetch hides from South America. It is amazing that such a small port in a remote corner of Cardigan Bay had such

LEFT
Conwy Castle
The great battlements of Conwy
Castle provide an imposing backdrop
to vessels moored at the quay, and
here backlighting has been used to
fling it into silhouette and so lose the
detail. Built in the late thirteenth
century, the castle was designed to be
provisioned from the sea. I have lost
many of the modern trappings in the
misty atmosphere. This is an oil
painting on canvas.

ABOVE
Trearddur Bay
On the western seaboard of
Anglesey, this bay is perhaps at its
best in the evening, particularly
when there is a glorious sunset.

Lleyn cottage
Scattered around the Lleyn Peninsula are many farms and cottages, clinging to the very edge of Wales. This one stands near Aberdaron. Turner Grey tinted paper has been used for this watercolour.

an influence on ship design, and that its seafarers enjoyed such an outstanding reputation for seamanship that was second to none, all over the world.

Across Tremadog Bay stands the brooding castle of Harlech, perhaps the epitome of every schoolboy's idea of what a real castle should look like. Perched dramatically on a crag 200 feet (61 metres) above sea-level it holds a commanding position. Built in the late thirteenth century by Edward I, it featured prominently in the Wars of the Roses. It was held for the Lancastrians by Dafydd ap Jevan ab Einion for some seven years until eventually he surrendered because of starvation. This is commemorated in the song 'Men of Harlech'. The castle was a popular subject with Sandby, Varley, Turner and Cotman.

Further down the coast, clinging to the very edge of the wild stark crags of the Rhinog mountain range, stands Barmouth. Scenically it is best approached from the east, down the estuary, which provides quite a spectacle as it opens out. Wordsworth described the estuary as 'sublime' and Wilson, Turner, Cotman and many other famous artists came to paint the views. Equally beautiful, if not quite so dramatic, is the Dyfi estuary, at what must be the southern limit of the North Wales coastline. The estuary is rich with a variety of bird and plant life, and is very different in character to the coast further north. The last time I visited Aberdyfi the river sparkled in pale afternoon sunlight, the distant mountains blurring into grey clouds. What more could an artist ask for?

LEFT
Barmouth
Cotman and Turner were two major artists who painted the view from Barmouth towards the craggy northern cwms of Cadair Idris. Here I have laid a wash of watercolour on Canson paper, delineating detail with a watercolour pencil. The highlights have been accentuated with white chalk.

OVERLEAF
Ballast Island, Porthmadog
This is a manmade island composed of stones from a great many countries around the world. Because the hinterland around Porthmadog could not support vast imports the slate-laden schooners would sail out with their loads and return mainly with stone ballast from wherever they had been. The stones were dumped here, and eventually grew into a large island, when a jetty had to be erected. The remains of the jetty can clearly be seen.

5

BISHOPS AND BITCHES IN NORTH PEMBROKESHIRE

Carregwylan
Ceibwr Bay has a savage rawness epitomized in these crags thrusting up like two sea monsters. It is hard to convey in a watercolour the sense of immense scale and presence that they impose on the viewer.

If you ever come across the sea from Ireland, heading for Fishguard, maybe you will be as lucky as I was when one morning a low mist hung over a sea lit by strong sunlight. Slowly the great unmistakeable shape of Garn Fawr appears through the haze, high above the Strumble Head lighthouse. Perched precariously on a crag rising out of the swirling surf, the lighthouse winks its beam every few seconds. This is the first sight you have of the Pembrokeshire coast, a coast of raw wild splendour, steeped in the romantic legends of Celtic folklore; a coast of spectacular cliff scenery, soaring stacks and golden sands, of fascinating wildlife, a glorious playground for those who love a natural untamed environment. Unlike so much of our coastline most of this coast has hardly been exploited commercially. Long may it stay that way. Every landscape artist has a place that fires his heart more so than others – Pembrokeshire is such a place for me. Though amalgamated into the larger county of Dyfed during the 1974 local government reorganization, Pembrokeshire's unique identity ensures that the spirit and name of the old county flourishes, whatever may be decided in Westminster.

Near the northernmost point of the Pembrokeshire coast lies Ceibwr Bay, a place of contorted rock strata – a place to be savoured when surely at its best – in the wildest weather. Walk south west along the coast. Two colossal stacks of sheer naked rock rear out of the sea close inshore where cliffs rise vertically some 200 feet (61 metres). These are dangerous cliffs. Never was I so nervous as when I walked along the top here watching seven-year-old Catherine like a hawk. Soon the intermittent flashing of the Strumble Head lighthouse punctuates the horizon just over thirteen miles ahead. After a mile the path descends past Pwll y Wrach, the Witches Cauldron, an immense collapsed blowhole at the bottom of which a tunnel admits the sea. The stream coming down the valley seems to panic just before reaching the sea, swirls crazily through a short deep chasm into a savage gash, down an underground passage and into the Witches Cauldron, a veritable Land of Styx where, like Juno, one might expect to confront the Furies, those terrible snake-locked goddesses. Beyond lies a stiff climb to impressive cliffs, in yards taking you from the underworld to the dizzy heights where you would expect to find soaring eagles. If you are lucky you may see choughs, but eagles are highly unlikely! From here a footpath can be taken inland to Treriffith farm, and hence back along lanes to Ceibwr.

The old harbour at Lower Town Fishguard is one of my favourite sketching haunts. Despite having to pick my way through oozing mud and the River Gwaun as it pours into the sea, I prefer it at low tide. Then the puddles left by the receding tide create fascinating reflections of the boats leaning on their sides. Green-tinged ropes and rusting chains add to the glorious confusion of ground detail. Always the optimum sketching viewpoint seems to be in the middle of deep clinging mud! Beyond the harbour wall, itself a feast of intriguing textures and colours, stand the cottages, neatly strung along the harbour in a manner that is distinctly Welsh in character. In the late eighteenth century at least fifty coastal trading vessels were based here. Gone are the days when it was an important herring fishing port, and it is now chiefly the province of the pleasure sailor, and youngsters pulling small crabs out of the water on the end of a line.

Carregwylan
This is the original pencil sketch, to which I added pencil notes.

Pwllderi, on the western side of the Strumble Head peninsula, has a supreme wildness that from the landward side is difficult to capture on film or canvas. Awkward angles diminish the sheer dramatic presence of the steep rugged cliffs stretching away to the south west. These lonely stretches of coast are interspersed with remote beaches ideal for smuggling, and not only in the dim past. On a wild night in November 1986 the fishing trawler *Minou* ended its long passage from Morocco and hove to off the small beach at Aberbach. Stealthily the crew loaded its sinister cargoes into dinghies. As they made for the shore, however, thirty-foot (10-metre) waves overturned the boats. Hidden along the shore in wait for the smugglers were customs and police officers, and so abortive was the mission that two of the gang had to be rescued from the pounding surf by the waiting officers. One and a half tons of drugs were recovered, and four days later the *Minou* was arrested at sea by a fisheries protection vessel.

On the beach at Trevine one evening I witnessed an amazing sunset with jagged rocks framing a savage foreground. After one sketch I walked across the rocky beach only to find that in my trainers the going was far too slippery. After crashing to the ground for the third time in the space of a few yards, I retreated up the beach, and traversed higher up on some firm gabbro. I then descended into a tunnel-arch beneath a rock the size of a warehouse. Halfway down I met the sea coming in, each wave crashing against the wall of the arch with a resounding slap, amplified in the confined space. I looked up. The scene transfixed me: the sun hung just above the horizon, framed in the craggy archway, a magical picture. The next wave hit me as I fumbled for my camera. Luckily the sun stayed up long enough for me to sketch it, and the sea didn't cause too many problems. As the moon rose I climbed up the path above the cliffs on the west side of the bay. Without warning a dark shape shot out of the undergrowth and stumbled along the path ahead of me. In the dim light I could see it was a small badger. Moments later there came a thumping in the undergrowth above, and down the hill came Mummy badger. Deftly she steered her little one into the bushes and to-

Lower Fishguard

Sunset at Trevine
Dramatic lighting and fang-like rocks ensured that I was kept busy on this evening – in fact until well after 11.30 pm when it was dark. When there is so much beauty one wonders which way to look next.

Cliffs at Abereiddi

Trevine archway
This is an original watercolour sketch, clearly indicating my extreme haste, for the tide was coming in. Although it appears placid enough the occasional large wave kept me on my toes. I was very lucky to find the sun setting in exactly the right spot. This was done on the same evening as the Trevine sunset painting.

gether they disappeared into the darkness. Then silence. I climbed a stile and walked a few yards. The moon shone high above Pwll Crochan to the west, with the isle of Ynys-fach barely visible in the pale luminous light. Although not easy to see, I did manage three sketches along the cliff before turning back, well contented with the evening's work. So often it is the most rewarding part of the day.

In a sheltered creek round the headland from Ynys-fach lies Porthgain which, until the mid nineteenth century, was of little significance. In 1849 work began to exploit the slate and granite resources – high quality granite from Porthgain was ideal for brick-making. A thriving coastal trade built up, mainly with ports in South Wales and Bristol. Slates were also brought by tramway from nearby Abereiddi, where the beach is exposed to the westerlies, and suitable only for small sloops and smacks. At times up to twenty sailing vessels would be crammed into Porthgain harbour during the late nineteenth century. After World War I the industry declined because railways were able to move slates from other areas more rapidly. The huge brick hoppers still stand today, forlorn, gaunt reminders of past glories, an intrusion into the natural landscape.

From Abereiddi to St David's Head the coast is dominated by the craggy outcrops of Penbiri, Carn Treliwyd, Card-ffald, Carnedd-lleithr and Carnllidi, resistant intrusive igneous rocks

St Brides
The end cottage on the left was formerly a chapel. It is said that when it was converted from being a chapel all the herring disappeared from St Brides Bay.

Vital Spark approaching Solva
Solva has provided me with an
enormous number of subjects, and I
have sketched this fishing boat many
times from different angles.
From the collection of the author

Dinas Fach
These huge rocks lie south east of
Solva and are viewed here from a
boat anchored in the lee of the rocks.

pillage, and live off the land. This they set about with a gusto as soon as they landed. Not many days before the invasion a Portuguese ship had foundered on the coast and so almost every local house around Pencaer had at least one barrel of Portuguese wine, which went down well with the *Légion Noire* – they had quite a party that night. The seventy strong Fishguard Fencibles thirsted to get at the French upstarts, despite being outnumbered twenty to one. A shower of bricks and bullets from the Fencibles would probably have been enough to strike terror into the hearts of the French ruffians, but Colonel Knox, the officer in charge, decided to await reinforcements. Whilst they mustered and muttered in Fishguard, however, the situation at Pencaer had become farcical. Farmers were trying to drive French soldiers out of their fields and buildings, and

losses occurred in both sides. One large Amazonian lady, Jemima Nicholas, set about the Frenchmen with a pitchfork. After capturing twelve she led them off to Fishguard guardhouse, then went back for more.

Late in the day Lord Cawdor of Stackpole arrived with about 500 men of the Pembrokeshire Yeomanry from the south of the county. After a long march the men were tired so battle did not commence until the next day. In the morning, the French watched as Cawdor approached from the south, and to their dismay they saw what appeared to be a large company of Grenadiers coming from Fishguard. These were in fact local women, dressed in their red cloaks and tall black Welsh hats, and said to be armed to the teeth with pokers, stakes, pitchforks and probably rolling-pins. At the sight of this great army Tate

Nolton Haven
One day someone arrived here to find the sea had turned red! Pink foam was being blown off the surf as firemen, coastguards and police arrived en masse. The colour was attributed to a drum of dye. This watercolour sketch was done as a sketching demonstration for a group of students, when the sea was behaving quite normally.

surrendered. Official historians tend to play down the part of the women, which perhaps smacks a little of chauvinism.

Halfway down Ramsey Sound, which cuts Ramsey off from the mainland, stand the Bitches, a reef of jagged rocks visible at low tide. These were said to have been formed by St Justinian who, fed up with the rat race, retired to Ramsey, and in so doing chopped off any possibility of pursuit by unwanted visitors, leaving only the Bitches as evidence of a former connection with the mainland. At times the roar of the tide-race is frightening, with a fine mist across the sound caused purely by spray thrown up by the agitated water. Despite the fact that the rocks could rip the bottom out of a boat in no time, two of my friends who run an outdoor centre in Twr y Felin at St David's dared one day to paddle a kayak over them. It not only worked,

but gave tremendous fun. This resulted in the lads forming an event called the Bitches Wild Water Rodeo, held on a spring tide to ensure plenty of water. The event has become a popular item in their calendar.

In summer, Solva, a haven on a truly savage coastline, is always crowded out with yachtsmen and tourists enjoying the beauty. The name Solva appears to be of Danish origin, meaning samphire, a plant that used to thrive here, although legend has it that the Vikings named the village in honour of one of their fairest of princesses. No matter how many times I sketch here there is always something new, and the village never ceases to fascinate. Although it has a difficult entrance, the harbour is the best in St Brides Bay – well sheltered from storms – and formerly maurauders – by the sharp curve of the

Jack Sound
Another pastel painting attempting to show the rough water in the sound. The scene was viewed from the boat journey across to Skomer Island.

Sea King 190

We arrived on the cliff top at St Brides and, gazing out to sea, could make out a grey insect-like shape approaching the coast. As we watched the grey shape gradually turned yellow. The radio crackled to life with the voice of Flight Lieutenant Jim McLeod, CO of 'B' Flight, 202 Squadron at RAF Brawdy. The air vibrated as the helicopter came in close for me to sketch her broadside on, with Jim keeping her poised in a hover position. Although on a routine exercise, they were happy to 'pose' her for me. Posing a helicopter was not something I had tried before, but the problem was made easy by using a coastguard radio. I relayed my instructions to coastguard Ralph George, who then passed them on to the helicopter, whilst senior coastguard Dutchy Holland ensured that in the excitement neither of us tumbled over the sheer cliff. Jim then brought Sea King 190 over some rugged rocks and again hovered in position whilst I sketched. The Sea King has an automatic hover facility, and the winch operator at the rear can operate the helicopter laterally from his position to enable more accurate positioning in difficult conditions. After a while Flight Sergeant Dave Spain, the winch operator, lowered his winchman, Flight Sergeant Vaughan Dodsworth, down the line, and this is the scene that is shown in the painting. The winchman is lowered into the sea, onto rocks or the pitching deck of a ship to recover survivors, and he has to keep practising this procedure throughout the winter as well as during the easier months. The fourth member of the crew is the co-pilot, who on this occasion was Flight Lieutenant Dane Crosby. Their professionalism and obvious love for their work came over very strongly, as is apparent from their impressive number of rescues. The painting has been carried out in oils on board.

David Bellamy

The *Garlandstone*

Built by the James Goss' shipyard at Calstock, this 75-ton ketch was bought by a Captain Russan of Milford Haven in 1909, who named her after the massive rock off the north side of Skomer Island. In 1919 she was taken over by Captain Andrew Murdoch of Gloucester who then operated the *Garlandstone* mainly between the Bristol Channel and Ireland. Most of the time Captain Murdoch wore a bowler hat, which helped to protect his head from knocks against the deck beams. During World War II his Irish crew were not too keen on crossing minefields and U-Boat infested waters and so naturally left the vessel on arrival one day in Ireland. With the help of a local boatman, Captain Murdoch hoisted the sails and set off for the Bristol Channel where he hailed a passing tug. The crew helped him take in the sails and he returned to Lydney. Later the vessel was bought by a Polish artist and seaman who published a little book featuring drawings of the *Garland-stone*. For many years she was part of the little museum at Porthmadog, and was eventually bought by the National Museum of Wales. I was lucky enough to track her down at Morwellham Quay in Devon where restoration was about to start on her.

From the collection of the Pembrokeshire Maritime Society, which was formed to promote and keep alive the maritime traditions of Pembrokeshire.

inlet. In the past Solva was an important trading port, trading in cloth and timber with Wexford. Limestone was imported and some of the limekilns can still be seen near the head of the inlet.

Near Solva lies the RAF airfield at Brawdy, home of 'B' flight, 202 Search and Rescue Squadron, their yellow helicopters a familiar sight around the West Wales coast. When I visited them in mid October they had carried out 139 call-outs since the beginning of January, and had rescued seventy-seven people and a dog. They are called out to an amazing variety of incidents, from large ladies to large ships, and theirs was the first British helicopter to arrive at the *Herald of Free Enterprise* disaster in Zeebrugge, with West Wales divers. On one occasion in Swanlake Bay an extremely large lady injured herself. Unfortunately she could not get over the stile to the waiting ambulance. No amount of heaving would get her over. Eventually a helicopter had to be called up to lift her over! One of the major rescues by the flight involved two Sea King helicopters. On the evening of 23 November 1986 Sea King 190 was scrambled from Brawdy to an incident off the Eire coast involving a Spanish trawler. Normal procedure in rescues to the west of Ireland is to land at Cork or Shannon to refuel. The helicopter was joined at Cork about an hour later by Sea King 191, and as

they awaited search area information a Mayday call came in from the 169,080-ton bulk carrier *Kowloon Bridge*. She had broken her rudder fifteen miles west of Fastnet Rock. Immediately both helicopters scrambled from Cork and flew into gales gusting to Force Eleven as they approached the stricken vessel in the darkness.

Rescue 190 went in first, and in seventy-five mph winds hovered over mountainous seas, with waves seventy feet (20 metres) high crashing over the decks of the great ship. Fourteen seamen were taken off without incident. Then it was the turn of Rescue 191, piloted by Flight Lieutenant Tony Gear, with fourteen more survivors to bring up. Suddenly disaster struck. As Flight-Sergeant Dave Spain lowered his winchman, Sergeant Barry Hunter, onto the pitching deck the *Kowloon Bridge* was thrust upwards by a gigantic wave. Hunter crashed against the ship, breaking bones in his left hand and badly jarring his elbow. Despite the pain he recovered himself, and then proceeded to take up the remaining crew. Soon all the sailors were safe aboard the helicopter. For this rescue the flight received an award for an outstanding rescue at sea from the Fishermen and Shipwrecked Mariners Royal Benevolent Society.

6
THE ARTIST AND
THE SLEDGEHAMMER

Sandy Haven
A watercolour on Turner Grey tinted paper. Sandy Haven was a favourite sketching location of the artist Graham Sutherland, who based many of his paintings on the rock- and tree-forms found in this spot. He admitted to being obsessed by the shapes in the mud here.

Off a remote stretch of the Pembrokeshire coast at the south-west tip of St Brides Bay, named after the Irish saint, Brigid of Kildare, stands Skomer Island. One of the most important seabird sites in southern Britain, it has up to 100,000 pairs of Manx shearwater breeding, plus great numbers of fulmars, storm petrels, puffins, guillemots and razorbills. In May and June the island appears misty blue with drifts of bluebells, tempered by a profusion of red campion, and, on the cliff tops, sea campion and thrift abound. The island is managed by the Nature Conservancy Council.

The short trip across to Skomer from Martin's Haven was Catherine's first taste of seafaring, and as we drew into the full force of Jack Sound she was not too enamoured by the twenty-five-foot (7-metre) waves, especially when the boat fell to the bottom of a trough. Her apprehension turned to measured glee as we shot up onto the crest of a wave. To take her mind off the waves we began a game of 'watch the birdie'. A shag obligingly skimmed across the waves like some feathered Exocet missile, amazingly never touching the crest of a wave, despite flying so low and with such a level course. Catherine was glad to reach Skomer, just as a single puffin shot past diving in a great arc and seemingly trying to emulate the shag, but its clown face and high trajectory hardly gave it the streamlined air of an Exocet. Skomer is certainly a lovely place to take a child, not just for the birds and scenery, but for the many seals which usually lie basking at the base of the Garland Stone at low water. Around seventy seal pups are born each year around the island.

From Skomer there are excellent views of Skokholm and Gateholm Islands, the latter accessible by walking across from the mainland at low tide. The names of these islands originate from the Norsemen. Beyond Gateholm on the mainland lies the magnificent beach of Marloes Sands, with great rocky ribs thrusting up out of the sand in places. The rock scenery from

Westdale Bay

An oil painting on canvas illustrating the jagged tooth-like rocks that could tear a ship apart in no time. The red cliffs of this bay reveal the powerful effect of erosion: one side seems to be crumbling into the sea.

Asgard II approaching Milford Haven

Whilst I was visiting the Milford Haven Coastguard Centre on St Ann's Head the brigantine _Asgard II_ sailed into view below us. After a mad dash by car across the headland I managed to sketch and photograph the vessel as she entered the haven. This beautiful sailing ship was built by John Tyrrell and Co of Arklow, Co Wicklow, for Coiste an Asgard, the Irish Sail Training organization. She is seen here approaching Milford Haven under reduced sail, her white sails dark against the backlighting.

Wooltack Point to St Ann's Head is outstanding. At Westdale Bay the effect of erosion on the deep red sandstone is evident for all to see. At the northern end of Westdale beach the broken rock looks as though it has been pummelled by some giant's mortar and pestle.

On St Ann's Head stands the coastguard station, commanding a magnificent view of the sea approaches to Milford Haven, though these days most of the work of the coastguard is done by radio communication and not from visual sightings. I was extremely impressed by the speed with which the coastguards can contact the rescue services: it is almost instant. Off the main control room there is a pollution room, which is manned whenever there is a major pollution problem, such as an oil tanker spillage. Many people have a distorted view of the work of the coastguard, and perhaps the image of an ancient sea-dog standing in a small white cliff top hut with a telescope in one hand, is not easy to dispel. The service was set up in 1822 to combat smuggling. By the mid nineteenth century the coastguards came to be regarded as a reserve force for the navy, but during World War I the service was decimated by the loss of three cruisers manned by coastguards. These days the service is highly sophisticated, enabling them to carry out their main role as co-ordinators for rescues at sea or on the cliffs.

Dutchy Holland, a genial ex-seafarer, has been a coastguard at St Ann's for some ten years, over which time he has witnessed many incidents, from the amusing to the tragic. Some of the questions he has been asked include: 'Does the tide come in at night?', 'What do ships do at night?' Incidents can run from vessels with engine failure to windsurfers knocking themselves out, someone trying to float across to Ireland on a lilo, cliff rescues of stranded climbers, and people cut off by the tide. Then there are the more mysterious reports from the public which occur regularly, usually relating to lights to seaward, various coloured flares and unidentified objects found on the beach. All of these need investigating by the coastguard. One rainy night a massive search was instigated when people at a dinner party reported seeing red flares out to sea: eventually it transpired that the 'red flare' had been the reflection of a cigar in the window. It is Dutchy's job to decide whether the lifeboat or helicopter is best in any particular circumstance. The regular coastguard service is backed up by auxiliaries, whose duties range from assisting in the coastguard centre to manning rescue companies with all the gear for cliff rescue, as well as reporting members who inform about problems around the coast. Dutchy recalls one rescue company who went to the aid of a courting couple on the cliffs, and the chap was rescued without his trousers! In August 1987 the rescue services between Barmouth and Llanstephan, the area covered by the Milford Haven Maritime Rescue Sub Centre, were called upon 144 times. The coastguards play a vital part in safety, not just for mariners at sea, but for ordinary tourists, and yet they face a constant threat of reduction of centres. Even the faithful old breeches-buoy and line-throwing equipment which have served them so well over the years have passed into retirement. These are fairly inexpensive pieces of equipment used by the rescue companies, and the argument is that the work can now be done by helicopters. What happens, however, if the helicopter cannot get close enough because of bad conditions, or has to be called away on another rescue? The Whitehall accountants are unfortunately too far removed from the real world to comprehend the need for safety. Rescues, perhaps, are not statistics, only deaths.

Across the entrance to Milford Haven from St Ann's stands West Angle Bay, connected to the pleasant village of Angle with its bay on the east side of the peninsula. The mixture of pleasure and working boats makes Angle an attractive sketching location. The best view of the village itself is from out in the bay – in deep mud at low tide! The Old Point House Inn on the shore at Angle was once the haunt of the notorious pirate John Callice. Milford Haven itself was said by Lord Nelson to be one of the finest natural harbours in the world. At the eastern end lies the great castle of Pembroke, and here in 1457 Henry Tudor, later to be Henry VII, was born. Some 486 years later on the other side of the castle wall, I first saw the light of day. Bringing up a baby in wartime Pembroke was no fun, according to mother, as it became an important target for the Luftwaffe. We had several adventures before I even became a toddler. Not that I recall any of it!

David Bellamy

ABOVE
Stack Rock
Once part of the mainland, this stack rises sheer out of the water. It supports many colonies of sea birds.

OPPOSITE
The Green Bridge of Wales
One of the geological wonders of Wales, this fantastic arch rises out of the water near the Eleugug Stacks in South Pembrokeshire. It is seen here with evening light falling across it.

The most southerly part of Pembrokeshire from Linney Head to Bosherston is alas used by the army's Castlemartin Range, access to the western part being denied completely except for a number of guided walks at specific times. The other part from the Green Bridge of Wales, including Stack Rocks and the fantastic rock scenery of Flimston Bay all the way to St Govan's Head, is open when the red flags are not flying. To have an army tank range firing live ammunition in the middle of a national park is nothing short of disgraceful. Obviously the army need to train somewhere, and they were here before the national park was designated. Arguments in favour of the range include the promotion of local employment, and amazingly the protection of wildlife and plants – the army makes great play of how it holds this land 'in trust for the nation', as though tanks and guns are necessary to protect the plants and wildlife! This has come about by the total absence of intensive farming methods, such as the use of pesticides and artificial fertilizers. Surely here is a marvellous opportunity to set up a National Nature Reserve to preserve this special area, and though it would still deny access to much of it, with ingenuity and imagination it could be transformed into an attractive site. Naturally it would cost money to move the army, but surely in the long term it is worth moving them out of the national park. In the meantime guided walks are a start, but something of a mockery to those who desire solitude when out walking, or want to study or sketch.

Further along the coast stands the Norman castle at Manorbier where Giraldus Cambrensis the chronicler and priest was born in 1146. Above the east side of Manorbier Bay stands King's Quoit, beyond which the walk towards Lydstep contains intimidating rock structures of great interest. I once did this walk on a stormy, misty day when fine spray fell on the watercolour sketches, imparting a fine mottled texture to them. Alas, once more at Old Castle Head we come up against the barbed wire and strident forbidding notices of the army. In the mist the headland looks more like a cold war outpost than a footpath in a national park. Although the Manorbier range has been much reduced it still hangs onto this small corner of Pembrokeshire. Skrinkle Haven, however, is now accessible. Steep

of ordovician age. Carnllidi is particularly impressive, especially when viewed from the south, where tiny cottages and farms seem to impart it with much greater proportions than its modest 595 feet (181 metres) would imply. Penbiri Hill and Carnllidi are well worth climbing for the views, the Wicklow Hills being visible across the Irish Sea on exceptionally clear days. In late spring and summer the flowers on Penbiri form a brilliant splash of colour. St David's Cathedral was founded by St David in the sixth century. Its position low in the vale of the River Alun helped to keep it hidden from raiders, although this did not stop the Vikings from burning down the cathedral in the eleventh century. It was rebuilt in the late eleventh century. The ruined Bishop's Palace stands in the cathedral grounds.

Overlooking the coast near St David's stands Trelyddyn Farm, where one day in 1780 Mrs Megan Williams was looking out across the sea through her telescope. She could see figures clinging precariously to one of the small rocks of the Bishops and Clerks group of tiny islands and rocks. Immediately she ran down to Porthselau, launched a boat into the wild seas, and rowed out alone towards the dangerous reef, some three and a half miles away. Not only were the sea conditions frightening, but the tide race down Ramsey Sound is extremely powerful, and once caught the boat would have been swept out to sea south of Ramsey Island. When she reached the rock after what must have been an exhausting row in a wildly tossing boat, she found seven men, survivors from a Swedish ship heavily laden with a cargo of iron. One sailor had been swept off the rock to his death. She then took them back to Trelyddyn and looked after them until they had recovered from their ordeal. Her achievement in rescuing these seamen was outstanding, and yet, amazingly, she was never made a national heroine. Her story deserves more than to be lost forever in dusty archives. Pembrokeshire folk are very modest about their achievements, which in other parts of Britain would be woven indelibly into the fabric of the folklore. Surely it is not too late to celebrate this remarkably brave and resourceful woman?

Thomas, Mrs Williams' husband, must have been quite a character as well. Formerly a sailor, Justice of the Peace, and High Sheriff of Pembrokeshire, he took a keen interest in shipping movements off St David's Head. One morning in February 1797 when out for a walk he caught sight of a squadron of four warships off the North Bishop Rock. Through his telescope he could see that they were flying British colours. The decks were crammed with troops. But he wasn't deceived: the ships were French. Sending a message to St David's, he then followed the ships along the coast towards Fishguard, and by late afternoon watched them drop anchor off Carregwastad Point, about two miles west of Fishguard Bay. The ships then disembarked 1400 troops, 800 of them ex-convicts, all under the command of an American colonel called Tate. Curiously, Tate could speak no French. The objective of the *Légion Noire*, as it was called, was to instigate a revolution against the English, and they had been encouraged to loot and

Moonlight, Pwll Crochan
Yet another painting resulting from that superb evening at Trevine. This is a pastel, viewed from the cliffs opposite Pwll Crochan.

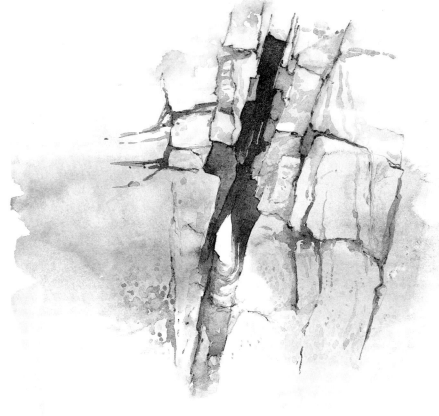

LEFT
Flimston Cauldron
This watercolour study on Turner Grey paper looks down into a spectacular gash in the limestone cliffs near Flimston Bay, with the sea crashing into the floor of the cauldron through rock arches. Kittiwakes shrieked and spiralled round the inside of this rock cauldron, in a way few seagulls would be able to imitate, whilst others clung to narrow ledges on the vertical cliffs. This is nature at her most impressive.

ABOVE
Church Doors Crevice, Skrinkle Haven
I just about managed to squeeze through here, and gain access to the adjacent part of the cove. The rock changes in texture and colour in horizontal layers, rather like the multi-coloured layer cakes my Aunt Win used to bake.

steps built by the army lead down to a small cove with a strange tall rock-window. The cove is the middle one of three in Skrinkle Haven. At mid-tide there seems to be nowhere out of this cove, the great vertical rock wall to the right appearing to be impregnable. On closer examination, though, there are breaches in the wall, and I was able to squeeze through one and make my way down a narrow slit to the adjacent beach, but not without having to scramble at the bottom over a rock pool like a clumsy crab. On the other side caves lead into the lower part of the limestone wall, and I spent so much time exploring and sketching that I was almost cut off by the tide, though this would not have been serious here, simply a longer walk back to the car. Geologically Skrinkle Haven is famous as the junction of old red sandstone and limestone.

Caverns Beach near Lydstep Head is a striking place, riven with cracks, caves, arches and impressive rock scenery. One of my visits here coincided with a wild storm. Massive breakers crashed against the rocks as ceaseless rain hammered down, creating a truly inspirational atmosphere. The soaring limestone towers at Skomar clearly show their vertical bedding, seeming to emphasize the fierce rawness of the cove, where one might well expect to find all the combined savage beasts of Greek mythology.

Tenby, or Dinbych-y-Pysgod, 'the little fortress of the fishes', in medieval times was famous for its herring fishing. Gradually it became an important port, trading with Ireland and the Bristol Channel ports. In the late eighteenth century it was handling about one third of Pembrokeshire's coal exports. One of the town's most fascinating characters was Charles Norris (1779–1858) the watercolour artist. He painted many scenes of the old harbour, and came from a prosperous landowning family. His habit of investigating anything with a hint of corruption made him a feared man to those indulging in anything underhand. On one occasion a landowner padlocked a

RIGHT
Skrinkle Haven
Only recently has the outstanding rock architecture of this cove become accessible, as formerly it was part of an army range.

David Bellamy

LEFT
Lydstep caverns
This arch is difficult to get at, but what a spectacular place it is on a wild day! This is a scene that conjures up enough terrors to be a fitting place for the great Kraken himself to have his lair. I could only reach the arch by wading, even at low tide.
From the collection of Jean M Thomas

ABOVE
Cliffs at St Govan's
So engrossed in my sketching did I get, that I was almost cut off by the tide. The first thing I knew about it was when I saw my palette bobbing up and down on the water! The cliffs behind the viewpoint are frequently festooned with rock climbers. Erosion is evident on a massive scale, for some of the blocks that have fallen off the cliff are the size of cottages.

gateway to a field, across which ran a public footpath. Norris wrote to the owner and the Town Clerk inviting them to meet him at the gate. As they turned up he produced a sledgehammer and proceeded to smash the padlock. He then flung the shattered padlock at the Town Clerk and as he departed suggested that it be filed amongst the town's archives. Tenby's most famous artist, of course, was Augustus John.

The Tenby of today is one of the loveliest harbours in Britain. Georgian and Regency buildings of colour-washed stucco stand in a huge sweep above the harbour, dominated by the graceful spire of St Mary's Church. The Tenby lifeboat station is one of the busiest in Wales, and has a fine record of lifesaving. One particularly outstanding rescue occurred on the night of 21 September 1953. That night, barely audible above the furious noise of a raging storm, coastguards heard the voice of the skipper of the *St Govan* lightship. The ship was rapidly filling with seawater as she lay broadside on to the wild seas.

Tenby Harbour
A quick watercolour sketch, showing
Goscar Rock in the background.

The pumps had broken down and she was helpless. In seas of such ferocity it seemed madness to ask the lifeboat to put out, but nobody hesitated. The maroons went up and within minutes the crew were assembled. At 9.42 pm the *John R Webb* shot down the longest lifeboat slipway in Britain and plunged into a seething sea with winds gusting to Force Ten. She had to cover some twelve miles to reach the lightship, and once the lifeboat pulled clear of the shelter of Caldey Island she caught the full fury of the storm.

Locating the vessel was a major problem, for without power she had no lights apart from an oil lantern hoisted into the rigging to guide the lifeboat. It was nearly three hours after launching that Coxswain Thomas Richards spotted a flare. As the *John R Webb* moved in the stricken vessel was rolling severely, a highly dangerous situation for the lifeboat. Richards closed in alongside the *St Govan* as huge seas swept over the vessel, lifting the lifeboat several feet above the deck of the lightship. For moments it seemed as though the small craft would be smashed to pieces on the lightship deck. Down came the lifeboat, narrowly missing the ship, and as the superstructure went under water the lifeboat was swept away, unable to get a line across. Richards took the lifeboat in for a second time and skilfully held her alongside using the engines to full advantage. A rope had been placed over the side of the lightship and bowman William Thomas caught it and made fast. But how long would it hold? The first man scrambled onto the lifeboat, but the rope parted just as the second jumped safely aboard. Again the lifeboat was swept clear. The coxswain took her in once more and another rope was caught. With the crew lining the port rail of the lifeboat the third survivor jumped aboard. Once more the *John R Webb* was thrust high above the lightship, only to fall down into the trough with the danger of the ship rolling on top of it. Soon all seven men were aboard the pitching lifeboat. She then swung clear and the coxswain headed back for Tenby. Coxswain Richards was awarded the Silver Medal by the RNLI for outstanding courage and seamanship, and the bowman William Thomas (whose son Alan is the present coxswain) and the motor mechanic William Rogers each received Bronze Medals.

7
SMUGGLERS, SERPENTS AND SAND

Llanstephan Castle
The castle perches romantically
above the estuary of the River Towy.

In 1956 the Gower Peninsular in south-west Wales became the first slice of Britain to be designated an Area of Outstanding Natural Beauty. And not without reason, for Gower crams a great deal of beauty into a very small area, the peninsula being barely fifteen miles in length and half that in width. Here are some of the finest beaches and cliff scenery in the country. The peninsula is steeped in legend and history and, not unnaturally, tales of smugglers. Brandy Cove and Pwlldu are reputed to have landed more smuggled goods than anywhere else in the Bristol Channel. Near Pwlldu stand two farms which were used to store contraband, and a tale relates how, one day, customs men arrived at one of the farms and found a cask of brandy in the loft. The officer in charge sent his men to get a horse whilst he sat on the barrel. Meanwhile, the smugglers made a dreadful din below as one of them bored a hole in the cask, going right through the ceiling, and thus emptying the barrel before the customs men returned!

Life around the coast in the eighteenth century must have been quite rough, and this is well illustrated by the arrival off Mumbles Roads of the naval tender *Caesar* in 1760. She was carrying a press gang looking for recruits. Not long afterwards the press gang of one lieutenant and twelve men came across two men on their way home from Swansea. The officer ordered their arrest, ignoring protestations, and the sailors fell upon the two lads, John Smith and John Voss. Smith quickly floored two sailors and Voss began despatching others. Quickly the naval force lost half its men, so the officer drew his cutlass, and from behind struck Voss a cowardly blow on the shoulder. This incapacitated Voss, but not before he had knocked out the lieutenant. At this point three friends arrived and quickly routed the naval gang. But the sailors' miseries did not end there. The gods were indeed angry when the sailors boarded their ship, for as they sailed down-channel a storm blew up,

Dylan Thomas's boathouse
At the mouth of the River Taf, this is a tranquil spot. As a youngster I used to fish in the Taf, and on some nights there would be as many as nine Bellamys on or in the river. This small watercolour was done on a Daler-Rowney watercolour board.

and mistaking their bearings, the vessel foundered on rocks at Pwlldu Head. Battened down below decks were at least sixty-eight victims of the press gang, apparently with their hands tied or handcuffed. They were given no chance of survival whilst some of the sailors managed to scramble onto the rocks to safety. Needless to say the naval authorities made no reference to the fate of the pressed men.

Three Cliffs Bay is beautifully spectacular, taking its name from three triangular interlocked rocky eminences. With the winding Pennard Pill leading the eye towards the bay it forms a classical composition without any real need for the artist to rearrange nature in any way. Hence it is popular with artists and photographers. High above the river stands the romantic ruin of Pennard Castle, starkly silhouetted on the crest of the ridge. Its history is obscured in the mists of time. Much of the building was engulfed in sand, said to be a curse put on the occu-

Gower Arch
Cut out of the cliff that gives its name to Three Cliffs Bay, this is a really impressive arch, especially when the sea is violently thrashing about on one side. Unfortunately it was not designed to have the better view looking out to sea!

Culver Hole
Culver Hole is unlike any other place
in the country. A long slit in the cliff
has been walled up, but for what
reason?

pants of the castle by the Tylwyth Teg – the fair people, or fairies. This was in response to revellers inside the castle attacking the fairies who were dancing outside.

Beyond the craggy limestone ramparts of Great Tor where it forms the western boundary of Three Cliffs Bay, lies the great curve of the sands of Oxwich Bay. My favourite part of Gower, however, is undoubtedly the wild sea-gutted line of cliffs from Port Eynon Point to Worms Head. Walking westwards the first feature reached is the mysterious Culver Hole, a narrow high cleft in the cliff, that has been walled up with a number of large openings. There is nothing else like it in Britain, and it is not known why or when it was built. Was it the stronghold of King Eynon? A pigeon-house? Or a smuggler's retreat? Legend has it that a passage runs from Culver Hole to the Salt House at Port Eynon, but no one seems to have found it. A length of marine rope dangled from the lowest entrance, which was some twelve feet (3.6 metres) off the ground. I pulled myself up the rope and as I scrambled inside there started a great thrashing and flapping up above as scores of pigeons took flight through the upper apertures. The gloomy inside stank with pigeon-droppings which littered the narrow steps up the side of the wall. Here and there lay broken eggshells. I climbed the steps, slippery with muck, glad to be wearing new boots with a sure grip – there was quite a drop to the bottom where even greater quantities of pigeon muck and beer cans awaited anyone unlucky enough to slip.

Frankly I was glad to get out of the place and into the fresh air of Overton Mere, a beach of jagged saw-tooth rocks cut into circular shapes by the action of the waves. It is dreadful stuff to walk across, and I thanked my lucky stars that I didn't have trainers on my feet. This is a place to linger on a pleasant evening when the beautiful rock pools reflect the western light against a backdrop of receding cliffs. To the west the limestone cliff scenery becomes increasingly impressive. In places the sea has gouged deep narrow channels at ninety degrees to the cliffs along the weaker fault lines. Some are over 650 feet (200 metres) long. I rounded a steep cliff to find hundreds of gulls perched on the rocks below. Immediately they all took off, filling the air with beating wings and loud cries. En masse

Wild surf, Gower

they circled a soaring limestone buttress above me, reminiscent of Monument Valley in Utah, only the rock here was light grey. As Jean Thomas puts it:

A living frieze
of gull-flecked, throbbing sky –
like fragments carved from spume
wave-tossed into the sea-hazed air
and patterning close, sombre cliffs
with white.

Approaching the next headland it seemed as though the path was about to disappear over a sharp drop. On reaching the edge I found the cliff fell away almost vertically to the raging sea, but an easy traverse along a narrow ledge eventually led to easier ground. This was a foretaste of what was to come. Now the scenery became truly spectacular, a wildness that I hardly imagined of Gower. The path in places almost slips off the edge, crumbling away with large fragile cornices left by the gouging effects of the tireless sea. Then the path climbed high, only to fall steeply down 150 feet (45 metres) the other side. Up again. Down again. A relentless switchback of limestone cliffs, like giant triangular bars running in from the sea. This is not a place for the unfit, and as I climbed the next slope I began to feel the effects of the climb. Although you can walk along footpaths on a more level plane further inland, you then miss the

Limestone cliffs
This watercolour sketch, done on the spot, illustrates the wild terrain between Port Eynon and Worms Head on Gower. You really have to be a dedicated walker to appreciate this stretch with its sharply angled strata.

Worms Head
Another pastel painting on Canson
paper. The head is accessible at low
tide.

spectacular cliffs, and therefore what really to me is the raison d'être for being there. I began to wonder how many more ups and downs there would be when suddenly the path disappeared altogether: sensationally over a precipice. No path, just the sea 100 feet (30 metres) below. Only gulls could pass this point. The rock looked too friable to consider climbing. I retraced my steps and then climbed up another path, then another drop. Near here in 1823 a skeleton dyed red with ochre was found in an almost inaccessible cave. Believed to be female it was named 'The Red Lady of Paviland', but on closer examination was found to be the skeleton of a Cro-Magnon man. In this scenery the Ordnance Survey simply gives up. Superb though their maps are, they make no attempt to depict the contours of this wildness.

Over the years these cliffs have seen a great number of ship-wrecks. One of the most famous was that of the *Roche Castle*, a trawler making for Swansea when she crashed into Paviland Cliff in January 1937. The Rhossili Lifesaving Apparatus Company had some difficulty manhandling their equipment to such a wild location, but their very first rocket shot over the vessel and was made fast. As the first two survivors were being hauled across on the breeches-buoy the trawler rolled over, throwing one into the air. He landed on rocks only to be crushed by the vessel as she came down on him. The remaining crew managed to get off without loss.

The sun beat down, making the going even more tiring. I longed to lie down and go to sleep on the inviting turf, so typical of limestone country, but Mum was expecting me for dinner. The scenery continued to excite all the way to Worms Head, with magnificent views across to North Devon. This is the spectacular culmination of a remarkable line of cliffs. At low tide the rocky foreshore can be crossed, giving access to the rearing contours of the Worms Head, more in keeping with a writhing sea serpent than a worm. As it happens, the word is derived from the Old English word meaning sea serpent. Nowhere else can you find such a gloriously wild coast ending in such a gloriously wild rocky sea-creature. A hissing, roaring sea-creature, as air is forced through a blowhole in the Head, where, on a wild day, to the uninitiated it might seem that Old

Nick himself is about to emerge. After all that I calmed down in a tea-garden in Rhossili.

For the artist Gower excels, though these days there is little to the west of Mumbles by way of boats to paint at close hand. One of the most accomplished artists to paint the shipping around Swansea and Gower was James Harris (1810–87). He was born in Exeter and moved to Swansea with his family eighteen years later. Working almost exclusively in oils, most of his paintings appear to be portraits of sailing vessels, with glimpses of the Gower coastline as a background. The small pilot cutters which used to put out of Swansea were favourite subjects with many Victorian artists. They would carry a pilot out as far as Land's End to guide ships up the Bristol Channel. Competition amongst the pilots was extremely keen. In 1898 steam cutters arrived in Swansea and put an end to these lovely sailing vessels.

Another piece of delightful coastline lies around Ogmore, south west of Bridgend. Nearby stands the charming village of Merthyr Mawr with its grey stone buildings and thatched roofs. Also nearby, in stark contrast, is the strange landscape around Candleston Castle, a fifteenth-century fortified manor house, now a neglected ruin. The castle itself has a foreign air about it, perhaps tropical, being almost surrounded by tall trees and engulfed by sand. To the west is an area of huge sand dunes. Though quite a slog getting to the top of the dunes it is worthwhile for the view back towards the castle, even if you get a welly-full of sand on each foot. Little boys love it – it brings out the Beau Geste in them. A maze of paths stretches across the sand dunes to the sea through bushes and shrubs and many varieties of wild flowers, including sea buckthorn with its vivid orange berries. I crossed this Welsh semi-desert on a hot August day, and was glad to jump into the sea at the end of the walk. The beach was almost deserted, whilst just across on the other side of the River Ogmore the beach was heaving with bodies.

Dunraven Bay and Trwyn-y-Witch are superb places for walking at any time of the year. A few years ago there was a beautiful line of trees above the cliffs, through which the sea glimmered, but sadly they have died, and though many trees

Coast at Dunraven Bay
Watercolour on Turner Grey. The
sketch for this was done in 1978
when it was evident that the trees at
the right-hand end were dying. Now
nothing remains of this once
beautiful line of trees.

Col-Huw Point
The drop below my viewpoint when
I did this pencil sketch was
absolutely sheer. Naturally I did this
one lying down!

still remain it has certainly lost something special for me. Foul deeds used to take place in Dunraven Bay, for according to legend a family of seventeenth-century wreckers operated here. They fixed lanterns to the horns of cattle on the cliff tops to lure ships inshore where they foundered on the rocks. Trwyn-y-Witch is a strange name, half Welsh, half English: I wonder why they didn't call it Trwyn-y-Wrach? South from this promontory lies a long stretch of beach with 200-foot (61-metre) cliffs. The cliffs appear to have been built out of bricks, for they are regularly layered in blocks. Cliff-falls are quite frequent here. On my last visit I found an incredible number of orange traffic cones on the beach: had they all drifted in from one vessel? Been dumped over the cliff by some pervert? Or had, as is more likely, there been a witches convention here the night before? Who knows. . . .

Col-huw, a break in the long wall of cliffs where the river flows down from Llantwit Major, was another site used by wreckers, and ships used to beach here to load and unload their cargoes. Nowadays the beach is easily accessible and one day with a friend I took a walk along the cliff tops from Col-huw. The sea sparkled where shafts of brilliant sunlight fell on the waves. I sketched as we lay in the grass gazing down the sheer drop of crumbling cliffs. This was not the place to dream, but I did, hypnotized by sea and atmosphere. Below us climbers practised on the vertical rocks of Stout Point. The Glamorgan Heritage Coast ends around the cement works at Aberthaw, which was once the most important port on this stretch of coast. Amongst other things it exported wool, butter, limestone and livestock, and had a great reputation for harbouring smugglers and pirates. Happily many old footpaths have been restored to give greater access to this lovely Heritage Coast.

Afterglow, Trwyn-Y-Witch
A cascade of water falls over the cliff on the right-hand side at Traeth Bach, and the friable strata of the cliff are shown in their almost brick-like structure.

8
WILDEST DEVON

Valley of Rocks

In North Devon the high moors of Exmoor sweep right down to the Bristol Channel, the rivers threading their way through delightful wooded gorges, or cleaves. Today little betrays the devastation that was wrought on the village of Lynmouth on that terrible night of 15 August 1952 when, after a period of exceptionally heavy rain, the cleaves of Exmoor disgorged a mass of water so great that it swept a large part of Lynmouth before it out into the sea. Boulders weighing ten tons were tossed about like peas in a cauldron. Cars, boats, people and houses were hurled before a wall of water twenty feet (6 metres) higher than the normal level of the East Lyn River. Even the Rhenish Tower on the harbour wall was demolished. All night the surging, roaring water rushed through the village whilst the terrified villagers hung on in the dark, desperately praying for dawn to come. Thirty-four people died that night in a disaster which captured the world's headlines. In the restoration of the village the striking Rhenish Tower was rebuilt in its original form.

One stormy night on 12 January 1899 a telegraph message was received at Lynmouth from Porlock Weir to say that a ship was drifting ashore and sending up distress signals. The crew of the Lynmouth ten-oared lifeboat *Louisa* did not even attempt to launch – the sea was violently crashing over the harbour wall, making it impossible. Coxswain Jack Crocombe decided to launch from Porlock, despite protests that Porlock was fifteen land miles away over extremely difficult terrain, along a narrow rutted lane awash with mud, and over two very steep hills. Slowly the lifeboat carriage was hauled up the 1063 feet (322 metres) of Countisbury Hill by a team of eighteen horses and many helpers. Through the gale and lashing rain they heaved the lifeboat across the desolate wastes of Exmoor. At one point the lane was so narrow that the three and a half-ton boat had to be taken off the carriage and pulled along on skids, whilst the carriage drove across the moor and met up with the lifeboat further along the lane. Hedges and walls were torn down, and trees felled to allow passage. One lady, awakened by the noise, looked out of her window at five am to find a lifeboat in her garden and the wall being torn down. They eventually came to Porlock Hill, one of the steepest roads in Britain. Gingerly the boat was brought down the hill into the village below. Some eleven hours after leaving Lynmouth they arrived at Porlock Bay to see the 1900-ton fully rigged *Forest Hall* perilously near the shore, holding on with both anchors out. She had been under tow from the tug *Jane Joliffe* when the cable snapped and the vessels drifted apart. Drenched to the skin and hungry, the tired lifeboat crew launched at six am. Fortunately the tug soon arrived, and the three vessels then sailed across to Barry in South Wales, joined by a second tug on the way. At Barry the lifeboatmen were thankfully given food – after twenty-four hours without any.

Above Lynmouth is the town of Lynton, the two being joined by a cliff railway. The railway, opened in 1890, is worked by gravity using a 700-gallon (3182-litre) water tank attached to each of the two cars. This was a favourite retreat of the poet Shelley, and he brought his sixteen-year-old bride Harriet Westbroook here in 1812. Their runaway marriage in Edinburgh had been precipitated by Harriet's unhappy home life, but she remained unhappy during the three years that they lived together. Their separation in 1814 was followed by Shelley's close friendship with Mary Godwin, but after she bore him a son in 1816 Harriet committed suicide in the Serpentine. Beyond Lynton stands the Valley of Rocks, an impressive place which I first saw on a miserable, rainy day, and sheltered behind a wall to sketch. A short climb takes you to the crest of the ridge, with the valley to the south and the cliff falling steeply down to the sea on the north side. On a clear day the coast of South Wales can be seen. Feral goats roam freely here, and the spine of the ridge makes an exhilarating airy walk. Woody Bay, further west, is aptly named. From here two tracks lead to Heddon's Mouth. Whilst the higher one is more level, the lower one holds more interest. When you turn the corner at Highveer Point the ground falls away sensationally some 700 feet (213 metres) to Heddon's Mouth down steep gorse, heather and scree-clad slopes. At the bottom is a pebbly beach with a restored limekiln that used to burn limestone brought over from South Wales.

West of Ilfracombe near Bull Point are Damage Cliffs, a particularly savage arena. Jagged rocks stick out of the sea like

LEFT
Lee Bay
Contorted cliff formations confront the viewer here, and these appear more dramatic in low directional lighting, when every ripple in the rock is accentuated to the full.

BELOW
Rhenish Tower, Lynmouth
The original tower was completely washed away in the terrible flood of 1952 but this exact copy was built in its place on the harbour wall. This work was done entirely using Derwent watercolour pencils, an excellent sketching medium.

fangs, waiting to rip the heart out of any vessel unfortunate enough to be driven onto this shore. From the lighthouse at Bull Point the coast sweeps round to Morte Point with its fast flowing tide rips. Just off the point is the fearsome Morte Stone, where five ships were lost during the winter of 1852, and countless others over the years. From here the coast turns south across Woolacombe Sands to Braunton Burrows, a place that seems alien to the Devon landscape. Here is a mass of sand dunes, a national nature reserve noted for many rare plants, one variety having the exquisite name of sand toadflax. War-games are played here, so watch out for the red flags. On the far side of the Taw estuary Appledore boasts a proud seafaring history, much of it related in the excellent maritime museum in the town. The boat-building tradition is still continued at Hink's Boatyard, where full-size replicas of ancient vessels have been built, including a Viking longship, a Roman galley and the *Golden Hinde*.

The wooded coastline around Bucks Mills and Clovelly pro-vides a complete change of character. The path meanders through woods of oak, beech and sycamore. Clovelly is unique. What a delight to walk – or rather, climb – through a village

Clovelly Harbour
The ancient stonework and rustic
timbers in the harbour walls
intrigued me. It was like stepping
back two centuries in time, and I half
expected to see a galleon appear
round the end of the quay. I arrived
here early, before the visitors, but
even so was still accosted a couple of
times. Using a small tape recorder is
a little inhibiting in a harbour, as
people tend to think you are talking
to yourself, but I find it useful to talk
and sketch at the same time
occasionally.

Storm near Bull Point
This is actually below Damage
Cliffs, and there were really wild seas
on the day I carried out the original
sketch. Needless to say, I became
quite wet in my efforts to capture the
mood of the scene. The
concentration of lighting adds drama
and atmosphere.

David Bellamy

without any cars. The cobbled main street, where sledges are used to haul things around, plunges down to the ancient harbour. To me the harbour, with its fourteenth-century quay of mellowing stonework and rustic timbers, is the crowning glory of the village. A fair-sized fishing fleet built up over the centuries, but was decimated on 4 October 1821 when, during a violent gale, twenty-four boats were lost and thirty-one fishermen drowned whilst fishing for herring. After an early morning arrival I sketched the scenes before the crowds descended, and then we retreated along the coast towards Gallantry Bower and had lunch sitting on the Angels Wings, an incredible wooden seat with a large canopy supported by wooden beams carved into the shape of wings, with further intricate carving all round. After the crowds of Clovelly, barely a mile or so distant, nobody stirred in this wood.

At Hartland Point starts the wildest part of Devon, a jagged, awesome coast, ravaged time after time by the fury of the Atlantic. On the day we arrived the lighthouse had been cut off by a rock fall, a graphic example of the instability of these cliffs.

The lighthouse, built in 1874, is perched below the great 325-foot (100-metre) high red cliff that is the cornerstone of North Devon. Within a few hundred yards lie the remains of the 960-ton Panamanian registered motor vessel *Johanna* which ran aground in the early hours of 31 December 1982. Although she was virtually intact on grounding, after eight days heavy seas had pounded in the starboard side of the hull, and within a further week the centre section had collapsed. Quickly she became a total wreck. She now lies in two rusting parts, her name almost obliterated. All the crew were saved.

The coast now turns southwards once more towards Cornwall. The footpath is easy going here, despite the wild coastline with parallel ribs of sharp rock jutting out into the Atlantic like rows of dragon's teeth. Lundy Island, once notorious for its pirates and smugglers, was visible as we walked southwards towards Damehole Point. From here we were treated to a magnificent view of the coastline stretching away to the south in a series of ever-fading blues. Oddly enough the high midday lighting was just right, throwing a backlighting on the coast,

LEFT
Cliffs near Gallantry Bower
The coast path to the west of Clovelly runs through beautiful woods, some 300 feet (92 metres) above the sea. At times I had to push through the undergrowth to check a view, and this was one such place. Unfortunately the only position from which I could obtain a reasonable view was up a tree. I climbed into the upper part of the tree, which was festooned with ivy, and carried out the sketch. As I moved my cramped leg the branch I was standing on broke – it was rotten. I checked my fall, then realized that half the tree was rotten. The ivy had covered the signs of rot. At this point I became very much aware that there was a 300 foot (92 metres) drop below me, and gingerly made my way down to the welcoming mass of briars and thorns.

Damehole Point
The ideal spot for a picnic, with a spectacular view towards Hartland Quay to the south. Although the rocks assume fantastic rugged profiles, the path itself is easy going, if a bit steep in places.

David Bellamy

ABOVE
Lifeboat off Clovelly
The lifeboat was moored outside the
harbour, as it is kept afloat all the time.

RIGHT
Hartland Point
Between Hartland Point and Bude
lies some of the most dramatic cliff

scenery in England, the grave of a
great many vessels. The wreck in the
foreground is the stern section of the
M V Johanna which grounded here

in 1982. Though virtually intact, she
quickly became a wreck through
pounding by heavy seas.

Hartland Quay
Viewed here from Damehole Point with early afternoon backlighting throwing each row of rocks into an ever-fading silhouette, rather like a theatre set. It has to be one of the most spectacular views in Devon.

and hence softening the detail and sharply defining the amazing contours of the rocks. The buildings at Hartland Quay were quite clear. This was Devon at its wildest and best.

Jagged dorsals carve the sea's soft shimmer,
gather, moveless; shoals of silhouettes
interrupt its smooth and silver glimmer,
unsettle poise with dark and hungry threats.

Jean M Thomas

During the age of sail Hartland Bay was one of the most terrible and feared coastlines in England for shipwrecks. At times in a bad storm vessels might even be blown across from the Welsh coast to founder on the rocks of North Devon. Even good weather wasn't a guarantee of safety, for on 3 August 1879 the French lugger *Maria Stella* sailed in good conditions onto the rocky shore at Blackpool Beach. The captain, on his way from Nantes to Cardiff, mistakenly thought the Hartland Point lighthouse was on the South Wales coast. Further along the coast, before Hartland Quay, a prominent ruin stands on the cliff top. This is the Pleasure House, said to have been used as a lookout for Barbary pirates during the seventeenth century. In those times the galleys from North Africa would sail up the Bristol Channel seeking slaves and plunder. One of the wildest characters to engage in wrecking, smuggling and all kinds of lawless pursuits in this vicinity was 'Cruel Coppinger'. Allegedly a Dane, he was wrecked on the coast during a hurricane in the mid eighteenth century, and then became leader of a gang of cut-throats. He had a rather strange way of making friends, for anyone who quarrelled with him had the choice of either joining his crew or being put to the sword. Apparently he was last seen boarding a ship offshore, and then disappeared into another ferocious storm!

Hartland Quay was once a busy port, and the building of it was financed by three of England's most famous sailors, Drake, Raleigh and Hawkins, in the sixteenth century. It now has an interesting museum, mainly devoted to the coastline. In 1887 a severe gale breached the harbour wall, which deteriorated until, in 1896, it was completely washed away. The new harbour wall was built in 1979. A short distance to the south of the quay St Catherine's Tor rises sharply, like a giant slice of half-eaten orange. One side is rocky as it rises from the seashore, while the other is covered in bracken and briars. It is said that at one time there was a chapel dedicated to St Catherine on the summit. If so it must have been one of the most precariously positioned chapels in the country. Not far from Hartland Quay Speke's Mill Mouth plunges over the rocks in a spectacular last fall before reaching the sea. It is a lovely spot to linger, ideal for a picnic. Not very much further south this really outstanding length of Devon coast ends at Marsland Mouth.

Morwenstow Church
A view of the church from the fields to the north east. After an easy stroll we came to the muddiest lane I've ever seen, where I spent most of my time carrying Catherine above the sea of mud. In this pastel painting I have emphasized the contrast of warm and cool colours.

9
MYTHS AND MINES

Wild seas north of Bude

The words that immediately spring to mind at the mere mention of Cornwall are 'smugglers', 'wrecking' and 'supernatural'. You have only to go into a bookshop in the county to see the emphasis that is placed on ghosts, witchcraft and the like. Yet so far, in all my visits to Cornwall, I've never seen a Cornish Pisky, headless horseman, or heard phantom hoofbeats! I still live in hope. Wreckers and smugglers there were, however, just like other coastal parts of the country, but in Cornwall their tales have become in many cases inextricably mixed with legend. Some historians tend to deny wreckers ever existed, perhaps not wishing to admit to the shady past, but not everything was rosy in bygone times. Existence was rough and hard for many, nowhere more so than in Cornwall where most of the county is exposed to Atlantic storms. Most of Cornwall believed in free trade, so smuggling to some was even a noble trade! When in dire poverty survival is paramount, and in ancient Cornwall there was often little choice.

Then there were those who tried to alleviate suffering and spread some goodness around. Men like the Rev R S Hawker, vicar of Morwenstow in the mid nineteenth century. The eccentric Hawker, usually dressed in fishermen's boots and jersey, spent much of his time writing poetry and recovering bodies from the shore to give them a Christian burial. His best known verse is from *Song of the Western Men*, a ballad about the protest of bishops against increased freedom of worship for dissenters. He built a hut of driftwood on the cliffs near Morwenstow, so that he could scan the bay in comfort. The walk from his hut northwards as far as Marsland Mouth passes some awe-inspiring rock scenery. It also has the advantage of affording a circular walk via lanes back to Morwenstow. We did this one glorious April day, when masses of daffodils bordered the path up to Morwenstow Church. When we arrived there were already several artists at work in the churchyard, though none seemed to be taking much notice of the daffodils. After some sketching we followed the path to Vicarage Cliff, which fell away in great chiselled precipices to a rock-strewn shore. From here to Bude this shore has claimed over 150 vessels. The route to the north took a switchback course over steep ground. Henna Cliff is a sheer 450-foot (137-metre) drop

to the sea, just about the highest sheer drop of a sea-cliff in England, apart from Beachy Head. On a clear day the Pembrokeshire coast is visible, but when we were there it was too hazy to see that far. Some of the steps cut into the hillside must have been designed for the Great Elasticated Long-Legged Man, and little Catherine had to put in a lot of effort to climb these, though she did so uncomplainingly. This is a walk to be done at leisure, for whatever the weather the scenery never ceases to excite. There is interest all the way to Marsland Mouth, the line of cliffs being at right angles to the strata, thus giving rise to rows of reefs running out to sea in great parallel lines.

Halfway to Bude, Sandy Mouth is the jewel in a contorted, primeval coastline. Here is a mixture of sand and rock, where vicious angled buttresses rise sharply skywards, a place where one might expect a Viking longship to land. Bude is one of the few havens of refuge along a coast of unrelenting rock, and on a stormy day many an ancient mariner must have been glad to see the place. In the days of sail, cargoes such as coal were dumped in the riverbed at high tide and then recovered at low water. Bude proved to be rather an idle station for the early

Morwenstow Church
A quick pencil sketch using the daffodil-bordered path to lead into the picture and the bare trees to support the church tower. This is a truly delightful spot on a sunny April afternoon.

Evening light, Marsland Mouth
This is the boundary between Devon and Cornwall, in the midst of some of the most impressive rock scenery in the country.

ABOVE
Mouls Island
The sharp rocks on the island echo those of Rumps Point, from where I did the original sketch in the dying minutes of a glorious September day.

After the tranquil serenity of Padstow, Rumps Point comes as a rude awakening to the senses, and I could not have asked for a better end to the day.

RIGHT
Crown Mine, Botallack
These buildings are perched on the very edge of the cliffs. From the higher engine-house the Boscawen Diagonal Shaft descended over 1500 feet (458 metres) beneath the sea. The miners below could hear the sea scraping the pebbles above. The top house worked the engine for hauling up the ore and miners, whilst the lower one operated the water pump.

David Bellamy

Preventive men, but in 1831 a 'suspicious sail' was spotted out at sea and so the Preventive boat set off in pursuit. Those on board the suspicious vessel appeared to act strangely, so the boat was boarded. Surprisingly no resistance was put up and the Preventive men brought their prize, the *Lord Nelson* of St Ives, into Bude. When she was searched only salt herrings were found, and the officers became a laughing stock. The skipper of the boat had in fact been rather pleased with the help that they had given his tired crew! When the schooner *Crystal Spring* was wrecked off Bude in August 1904 she was auctioned off: her rudder sold for 1/6d, boat 9/-, steering wheel 14/- and the hull, spars and masts for ten guineas.

At High Cliff, south of Bude, Cornwall's coast reaches its highest point at 731 feet (223 metres), but as the cliff drops to the sea in a gradual slope the impression is less dramatic than some of the lower cliffs to the north. The sharp point of Cambeak presents a wild sensation of plunging dizzy rock faces, and care is needed by any explorers. With a great sweep downwards the cliff nearby pulls out of its dive just above sea-

level, to end in a crag-girt rock arch. This point is well worth a visit. Boscastle, I find, is one of the most compositionally awkward places to paint on the whole of the Cornish coast. Trying to capture that twisting approach into the harbour is an artist's nightmare. The harbour wall is a splendid structure of stone and seaweed textures. The slate-rimmed channel must have been quite a trial to many a ship's captain in the days of sail, particularly in wild seas. Trying to marry up harbour and entrance successfully in a painting is not easy. The village, though full of tourists in summer, retains tremendous charm, and even includes a museum of witchcraft.

Soaring cliffs and high stacks, the rock-knotted remains of former parts of the mainland, are a feature of the coast from Boscastle to Tintagel. The scenery is gripping and if your blood warms to awesome, unyielding rock this is the place for you. Rocky Valley, in the midst of all this wildness, begins benignly enough from the coast road below Trevethey, but quickly turns into the craggy gorge that its name suggests. Halfway down a delightful waterfall tumbles over the rocks,

RIGHT
Boscastle
Boscastle Harbour is an awkward place to get a satisfactory composition, but the scenery is imposing.

OPPOSITE
Sandy Mouth
This place is best visited when the tide is out, so that you can make the most of the cliff scenery. This is a watercolour sketch painted entirely with Payne's Grey.

and nearby stand ivy-clad ruins. Cut into a rock wall behind the ruins are ancient maze carvings. Thereafter the valley becomes truly wild as it disgorges its twisting tortured stream into the sea near Long Island. Primroses, buttercups, violets and sea campion were rife here on the spring day I explored this spot. The walk up the valley above the coast road is a pleasant ramble through St Nectan's Glen.

Tintagel of course is steeped in the Celtic legends of King Arthur. Should the great folk hero return from his many resting places in England or Wales to free the country from tyranny, he will probably recoil in horror at the shops full of plastic sentimentality that overwhelm the visitor to the village. Out on the twelfth-century castle remains, however, raw nature thankfully dominates anything that man has imposed on her. The atmosphere of the site is impressive, the drops from cliffs to sea fearsome, and the views from the top superb. In places it seems to resemble an Inca ruin, perched high above 300-foot (92-metre) cliffs. Formerly the inner ward on the headland was joined to the mainland by a drawbridge. The

artist may need time to walk around and absorb the atmosphere sufficiently before getting down to work.

The countryside in this part of Cornwall never ceases to please the eye of the landscape artist: old cottages with crazy curves, drystone walls in zigzag herringbone courses of stone, wind-clipped bushes bent into weird shapes, and massive flat stone slabs built as walls for outhouses. One can only hope that the trappings of commercialism do not spread further to spoil the very thing that many come to see: the natural beauty of this lovely corner of England. Between Tintagel Island and Trebarwith Strand much slate-quarrying was carried out in the seventeenth and eighteenth centuries. At Penhallic Point slate was lowered by horse or donkey whim 100 feet (30 metres) down the cliff onto vessels moored below. This must have been rather a precarious occupation, especially in anything other than calm seas.

The origins of Padstow go back to the arrival of St Petroc, the Welsh missionary, in the sixth century. He founded a monastery here. In the days before railways it was the most active port on the north coast of Cornwall. Over the years the River Camel became increasingly difficult to navigate with its dreaded Doom Bar silting up. This notorious sandbank, the graveyard of hundreds of sailors, stretches across the mouth of the estuary. Legend has it that a local man shot a mermaid, whereupon she put a curse upon the place in the form of the sandbank.

At St Agnes Head the names Wheal Coates, Wheal Kitty and Wheal Freedom betray the fact that we are in the midst of mining country. 'Wheal' is a corruption of the Cornish word 'huel'. The crumbling engine-houses stand as stark cliff top reminders of the days when these were tough mining communities. Much of the natural landscape was devastated for miles in the way that open-cast mining does today, a savage blight on the scenery. Time and the forces of nature are returning the environment back to its original form. Artists and photographers have been quick to realize the demand for pictures of a Cornish engine-house – invariably captured silhouetted before a sunset. Some of these buildings are being preserved and act as a fitting memorial to the hardships and dangers faced by the

Mousehole at night
As I sat sketching on the sand in the dark something furry touched my sketching hand. It was a cat, and she stayed with me all the time I did this sketch. A Karisma watersoluble graphite pencil was used with a wet brush.

10
ALL AT SEA

Kynance Cove
Spectacular plunging cliffs of varicoloured rock make this cove one of the most popular in Cornwall. The air was full of birds and helicopters, as the navy played aerial 'Ring O' Roses'.

Land's End might be the most popular place in Cornwall, but to me it is a place to pass through quickly, for although the scenery is marvellous the trappings of commercialism are all too apparent. Half a mile to the south the cliffs become even more impressive. Only a handful of Land's End tourists get this far. The southern coast of the Land's End peninsula is one of the finest, with castellated granite walls and towers perched high above the surf. Carn Boel, Carn Lês Boel, Tol-Pedn-Penwith and Hella Point are all dramatic headlands with striking rock shapes. The coast walker is well rewarded, all the way to Mousehole. Penberth won my heart. No commercialization, just a few houses tucked together in a little cove with a smattering of gaily painted boats and a massive old capstan, once used to haul the larger boats up the granite slipway.

From Mousehole the vast arc of Mount's Bay is visible, stretching eastwards to the Lizard. In the days of sailing ships this bay all too frequently became a trap to any vessel caught in an onshore gale. With reduced canvas and violent buffeting by a heavy sea they might not make any headway, and even be steadily pushed back. If the vessel was far enough out to sea she might manage to clear the Lizard and reach Falmouth. Anchors would be dropped in an endeavour to hold the ship, but in such conditions these would slowly drag until the ship struck a reef, or else the cables would snap. The last big sailing ship rescue in Mount's Bay happened during a heavy gale in December 1911 when the barque *Saluto* from Christiansand was being driven towards rocks near Perranuthnoe. The Newlyn lifeboat *Elizabeth and Blanche*, a sailing and pulling boat, took off the entire crew with great difficulty, having to use their oars for the final approach. She pulled clear just before the barque hit the rocks and broke up. As the lifeboat entered Newlyn harbour she was greeted with tumultuous cheering from the large crowds, whilst the Salvation Army band played 'Oh God Our Help in Ages Past'. A measure of the success and

LEFT
Gweek
Watercolour and brown watercolour pencil sketch, done on the spot. This is a lovely branch of the River Helford.

RIGHT
St Michael's Mount
This is one of the less painted views of St Michael's Mount, viewed from across Mount's Bay and depicting the craggy western façade of the island.

courage involved in this rescue is the fact that a Lowestoft steam drifter also went out to help and had to return to port for fear of capsizing.

But not all attempted rescues end up that way. On Saturday, 19 December 1981 one of the most tragic sea dramas of modern times unfolded. In the evening a violent Force Twelve storm, gusting to ninety knots or more, was blowing when the Dublin-registered coaster *Union Star* reported engine failure about eight miles east of the Wolf Rock lighthouse. She began drifting towards cliffs four miles south east of Penlee Point. Immediately a Sea King helicopter was scrambled from the Royal Naval air station at Culdrose. On locating the powerless vessel the crew tried to take off the eight people on board, but in fifty-foot (15-metre) waves, hurricane force winds, and a wildly pitching deck, it was an impossible task.

Just after eight pm the Penlee lifeboat *Solomon Browne*, a forty-seven foot ($14\frac{1}{2}$ metres) Watson class boat, set off into the dark fury of the storm. Coxswain Trevelyan Richards headed towards the *Union Star*. The massive, almost vertical waves tossed the little lifeboat around, and it was in these near-suicidal conditions that she approached the coaster. As she came alongside the vessel a huge wave caught the lifeboat and lifted her high above the *Union Star*. As the *Solomon Browne* came down she landed on the deck, then slid off the coaster backwards into the sea. Undeterred, the coxswain took her in once more. Again, a massive wave caught her and she was thrown bodily across the hatch covers of the coaster like a piece of driftwood. How the lifeboatmen on board must have taken all this hardly bears thinking about, as the *Solomon Browne* again crashed into the raging sea. But they were still in control, and in the true spirit of the lifeboat service, game to carry on. The helicopter crew hovering above could hardly believe their eyes when Trevelyan Richards, without hestitation, once more

Falmouth tosher and yacht
These two rapid sketches were done from the yacht *Caenswood*, again using the Karisma watersoluble graphite pencil with water. This medium is excellent when space is lacking and a quick simple sketch is needed.

took the lifeboat alongside. This time she managed to stay against the ship's side long enough for four survivors to jump into the lifeboat. The *Solomon Browne* crashed violently into the side of the coaster, but still seemed to answer to the helm as she pulled clear. A message crackled through from the lifeboat radio to say that four people had been rescued. There were still four more to be taken off, and in driving rain visibility was almost nil. Once again the gallant lifeboat swung round, damaged, but determined not to give up. Watchers strained to make out something in those foaming seas. A few minutes later the lights of the *Solomon Browne* disappeared. There was no radio contact. Trevelyan Richards and his brave crew had perished.

Wreckage of the lifeboat was washed into Lamorna Cove that night. All eight lifeboatmen died together with the entire crew of the *Union Star*. An idea of the force of the sea that night is illustrated by the fact that the Sennen Cove lifeboat was unable to force its way round Land's End, and the Lizard-Cadgwith boat which helped in the search for survivors returned to her station with part of her guard rails and bulwarks flattened and a leak in her hull. Coxswain Richards was awarded a Gold Medal posthumously, and each of the crew awarded a posthumous Bronze Medal by the RNLI.

Being a man of the mountains, with little idea of being at sea in a sailing craft, I felt it was essential to get a true feeling of what it was like. Not without a little ambivalence I approached the matter. On one hand I wanted the weather to remain kind to sketch at sea, yet hoped for a little wild weather to experi-

Caenswood **heeling to starboard**
In this rough sketch I tried to capture the feeling of the spray hitting the yacht. This was done on the first day at sea when conditions were fairly easy.

Frenchman's Creek

The original sketch was done from midstream in an inflatable, really the best position for sketching the creek because the heavily wooded banks offer very limited vision.

Gull Rock

Another view from afloat, which I sketched whilst the girls were reefing the mainsail. The boat here was in the lee of high cliffs, but once out the other side of Gull Rock the waves really hit us as we beat into the wind.

ence boisterous conditions. Such an undertaking did need an expert to be in charge. I didn't know the difference between a painter and a shroud – in the nautical sense that is. Linda, who was to join me on this trip, had sailed the high seas in a yacht, but to get close to the subjects surrounded by dangerous rocks we needed local knowledge, and so approached Jan Robson of Mylor Sailing School near Falmouth. Having done a transatlantic crossing, sailed in the Bahamas, the Caribbean and round the Outer Hebrides among other places, Jan had also done much inshore fishing out of Falmouth with her husband, both longlining and crabbing. She was therefore ideally suited to the task.

Jan's yacht *Caenswood*, a Sadler 25, impressed me with the ingenuity of its design. Everything fitted so well: not an inch was wasted. The water was fairly calm as we edged out of Carrick Roads into the open sea and set course for the Manacles, those treacherous rocks off Porthoustock where hundreds of ships have foundered. Sketching proved easy in these conditions, with the sunlight highlighting the water, and many craft around to use as subjects. As we drew nearer the Manacles bell buoy tolled its mournful clang, warning sailors of the fearsome reefs that lay inshore. There is a channel through the Manacles, known only to local fishermen, and this was used once by a Falmouth packet when being chased by a French warship. The packet sailed through the channel without mishap, but the French ship hit the rocks and sank immediately. Another incident happened in 1636 when some vessels were peacefully fishing near the Manacles. Seven fishing boats were captured by Barbary pirates and some 240 men were taken off to slavery in North Africa.

We tacked back to the River Helford and into a strong wind with a mass of sailing craft at moorings. Once in the river we adopted shorter tacks with sharp changes of course. At this point sketching became quite a challenge, with bodies and ropes flying about in all directions. With all this mayhem going on around me I continued sketching, whilst the girls did all the hard work. My excuse was that we would almost certainly have collided had I been involved in such tight manoeuvres. At the end of a string of yachts we picked up a mooring. Once fast, we lowered the dinghy and rowed into Frenchman's Creek whilst a glorious evening sun beat down. The creek was immortalized by Daphne du Maurier in her novel of the same name. Far up the creek, away from the crowds, I shipped the oars and sketched whilst the boat drifted slowly along. Unfortunately the freeboard on the inflatable was virtually non-existent, and as I altered course it shipped a lot of water, which made my trousers extremely wet. The banks are hung with dense trees and it was along the eastern bank here that Catherine had her first real 'walk' at the age of one on her Dad's shoulders. We rowed back to the yacht in idyllic conditions.

Next day the sun rose in a spectacular blaze against sombre grey clouds over the estuary of the River Helford. The *Caenswood* slipped her moorings, and with a fresh breeze behind us, sailed serenely downriver. We had little forewarning as to what lay ahead. Soon we were making good progress sailing parallel to the coast on an easterly bearing for Dodman Point. Jan changed the working jib for a storm jib, a much heavier and stronger sail which would withstand stronger winds. Did she know something I didn't? A following sea thrust us along at an exhilarating speed. Off Porthmellin Head the sea, with a greater fetch here, began to roughen. The wind increased and soon we were ploughing through deep troughs. No other vessel could be seen anywhere in sight. It was my turn at the tiller as we approached Gull Rock off Nare Head, my next sketching target. As I brought the boat around to head inshore she was caught by a wave and heeled over at an alarming angle. I couldn't get her back on an even keel – were we going to capsize? Bellamy wasn't used to this sort of thing. Happily she righted herself after what seemed ages.

Linda took over the helm to enable me to sketch. Should I do a Turner and tie myself to the mast? No, Jan had a better idea, and produced harnesses. These are used when things get really wild. My thoughts were rudely interrupted by the great rock confronting us. Gull Rock reared out of the sea at an oblique angle, bristling with a combed crest that held the viewer's gaze. I managed a number of quick sketches, then Jan was calling for an extra hand. Once more I took over the helm as we hove to near the rock. The girls reefed the mainsail to reduce the amount of canvas that would be exposed to the fierce wind on our return to Falmouth. Too much sail in storm conditions can topple a yacht. Storm conditions, I asked myself quietly – what were we doing out here in storm conditions? I began to question the wisdom of it all, to myself. In all this self-argument I inadvertently 'went about' as they say in nautical places, having allowed the wind to catch the jib, and this apparently meant we were rapidly heading for the rocks. Linda, ever-watchful of my helming, took over the tiller to allow me to take my mind off our potentially dangerous position by doing some more sketching. By now I had one eye on the sketchpad and the other on my lifejacket. Gull Rock is one part of the reef that is visible but, as Jan said, 'it's the bits you cannot see that you worry about'.

The rocks rushed up, their jagged, hungry mouths
held pools with seaweed tongues that gurgled death

Jean Thomas's lines seemed too apt for comfort. Jan completed the reefing and we had now reduced as much sail as possible. From the lee of the high cliffs we made our way round Gull Rock once more. All was well until we drew clear of the shelter of the rock. The sea then hit us with one huge wave after another. We beat into the wind – sailing as close as possible to the direction of the wind so that we didn't have to tack too far out to sea. The sea, by now a Force Seven, showed its more savage side, and we were sailing into the teeth of it. Wave after wave crashed against the starboard bow of the yacht, throwing spray over us time and time again. You would see one coming, duck, and then immediately be caught by a second wave as you looked up once more. Quickly the salt water got into my mouth and eyes. It made me wonder how fishermen coped on long sailings in worse conditions. I seemed to be forever wiping salt off my lips. At times the craft heeled over violently, with water coming over the gunwhale as it seemed to thrust below the surface of the sea on one side.

We watched the sea carefully, as the submerged reefs around Gull Rock have claimed a number of victims. One such was the four-masted schooner *Hera* of Hamburg which, in 1914, was bound for Falmouth from Chile. She missed the St Anthony light and struck a reef by Gull Rock. Within ten minutes she sank, but nine of the crew clung to the rigging, which stuck out of the water. Thankfully her flares had been seen by coastguards at Porthloe. The Falmouth lifeboat put to sea, towed by a tugboat. From the cliffs the shore rescuers could see nothing in the pitch blackness. Close to Gull Rock, Samuel Hingston, the lifeboat coxswain, slipped the tow, but even though the lifeboat went past fairly closely a number of times the survivors could not be seen in the dark. For four hours the survivors clung onto their precarious position a mere few feet above the clawing sea. Then the first mate was washed away, followed by the second mate. As the lifeboat went past yet again one of the men blew a whistle that the first mate had given him before he drowned. Luckily it was heard by the lifeboat crew. Even as the lifeboat approached two more desperate men slipped to their deaths, but five miraculously managed to hang on until help arrived. In all nineteen lives were lost.

It took some considerable time for our wave-battered yacht to come level with the St Anthony light, after many long tacks. Even then the beating into the wind seemed endless, ending up with a lot of minor tacks as we came into Mylor Harbour. Coming into a crowded harbour under sail demands superb and confident seamanship, and here Jan really showed her skill. It had been a marvellous experience and we had all enjoyed it, even more so now that we were back on land. The River Fal of course is a sailor's paradise. The last boats still working under sail survive here due to a local by-law which prohibits dredging for oysters with powered boats. The reason for this is that a motor boat would quickly finish off the oyster beds. Sadly the oysters are in decline and many feel that this is being caused by certain chemicals in the anti-fouling paint used on hulls. The working boats only operate during the winter months. Some of the craft, built using iron nails, without any brass or copper, are well over a hundred years old. By comparison, more modern yachts built of wood have endless trouble.

Falmouth was famous for its Packet Service, set up in 1668. The vessels were fast, lightly armed ships carrying the King's mail, military and naval despatches, passengers, and bullion,

ABOVE
Brixham trawler at Tregatreath boatyard
The battered hull of this old Brixham trawler was recovered after being smashed on Newlyn Quay, and awaits the day it will be repaired. On the right is *Shadow*, a Falmouth working boat about 110 years old.

Many of these working boats were built by Terry Heard in this boatyard, and it is recognized that without the boatyard the working boats would not have survived. Today the yard is run by Martin Heard who is continuing the traditional work carried out by his father.

RIGHT
Polperro
Arriving at Polperro in the middle of the tourist season was perhaps not terribly wise, but sometimes circumstances dictate events. I soon lost the crowds by jumping into the harbour – at low tide, I hasten to add, and sat in the middle sketching

this view. The artist really needs quite some time at Polperro, as there are so many intriguing angles. Also it is a good idea to see the place at high and low tide.

Looe
This view is looking across at the
western town from the quay, which
smelt strongly of fish. The original
watercolour sketch is shown here.

and in many cases illicit cargoes. Initially they operated to Northern Spain and later extended the service to the West Indies and America. Although under strict orders not to start a fight, they were regularly attacked, as they made rich prizes. Many of them defeated superior enemy ships.

Large ships still come into Fowey, which developed slowly as a port in the twelfth century. Before this ships would sail upriver to the sheltered waters of Lostwithiel. Trade increased rapidly, mainly with the ports of Brittany. In 1337, during the Hundred Years War, nineteen ships were provided by the port. When England and France ceased hostilities the men of Fowey continued the battle, waging raids on the French coast. One Fowey pirate seized fifteen ships off Brittany in 1469. When the king tried to stop this mayhem his messenger was sent packing with a flea in the one ear he was allowed to keep. Two blockhouses were built, one either side of the harbour entrance, and from these a great chain was stretched across to prevent a surprise attack by enemy ships. Nowadays Fowey is tranquil.

The coastline from Polperro to Plymouth Sound was at one time rife with fierce encounters between smugglers and Revenue Men. At Polperro the first Preventive boat was established in 1801, but the officers lived on an old hulk moored in the harbour, as no one would house them. On the harbour wall stands a beautiful harbour light, dedicated to the memory of the watercolourist Jack Merriott, who loved Cornwall. One of the greatest concentrations of smugglers congregated at Cawsand and Kingsand, despite the close proximity of the naval presence at Devonport and many customs officers in Plymouth. Even some of the customs officers themselves became involved. When things got too hot the smugglers would sink their kegs and recover them when the coast was clear. Not only did they risk capture or even death in confronting the Preventive Service, but they also had to face the hazards of a night landing in a dangerous rocky cove, often in rough seas. No doubt many of them did it for the thrill of adventure as much as for the reward.

Tregatreath boatyard, Mylor Creek
An unusual composition for me, but one that brought memories flooding back of when I used to visit my father's workshop in Narberth. Knee-deep in shavings, he would always greet us with a smile. These days the boatyard mainly builds glass-fibre craft, but repairs wooden vessels as well.

Sutton Harbour, Plymouth
From here the Pilgrim Fathers sailed to America. Although I have visited this spot many times, on this raw November morning I found the positions of the fishing boats just right, with the fishermen tending their nets adding to the interest of the composition. In a painting it is best to have people actually doing something, rather than simply posing. The trouble is that people never seem to be doing the right thing when you want to sketch them: they either look awkward, adopt a pose that looks wrong in a painting, or it defies explanation, or at times looks downright perverse! Trying to find fishermen to actually look as though they are doing something fishy is asking rather a lot.

11
THE CRUMBLING COAST

Rocks near Bolt Tail

The variegated colours in the water intrigued me in this unusual composition. I rarely paint from a viewpoint looking almost straight down, but the manner in which the rocks twisted downwards towards the white-foamed surf also caught my imagination.

When I first visited Sutton Harbour, the old port of Plymouth, the schooner *Kathleen and May* lay moored up against the quay, forming a marvellous composition. It was from here that the Pilgrim Fathers sailed to America in 1620 in the *Mayflower*, and Hawkins, Drake and Raleigh began their great voyages. The harbour is adjacent to the Barbican which gives a flavour of what old Plymouth must have been like before being heavily bombed during World War II. The French also tried to alter the face of the town in the fourteenth and early fifteenth centuries by trying to burn it, though without much success, so stoutly was it defended. For the siege of Calais Plymouth provided twenty-six ships, and of course it was from here the English fleet sailed to engage the Spanish Armada.

Off Wembury Point the Great Mew Stone is visible, a barren hunk of steep rock to which in 1744 a man was sentenced to exile for seven years. Mew is a common name, meaning 'gull' and there are many Mew Stones, including one in Pembrokeshire. From Dartmoor four lovely rivers, the Plym, Yealm, Erme and Avon flow through the South Hams, the last three forming beautiful estuaries on a coastline that alternates between wild rocky shores and lovely sandy beaches. Though not nearly as savage as the North Devon coast around Hartland, it has been the scene of a great many shipwrecks. The villages of Noss Mayo and Newton Ferrers stand on opposite sides of a fjord-like creek near the mouth of the River Yealm, an attractive spot for the artist. The Erme estuary is also scenic

Wonwell
At the mouth of the River Erme, Wonwell is a lovely spot, and this was one of the few occasions that Catherine got out her bucket and spade, whilst I sketched. The tide receded leaving hundreds of gulls pecking at the stranded morsels on the beach. At low tide one can wade across here to Mothecombe.

and peaceful, even in mid summer. It is quite an awakening to walk from the tranquillity of Wonwell on the eastern side to Bigbury-on-Sea where in season there are usually huge crowds. Opposite Bigbury-on-Sea is Bantham, a hamlet of thatched cottages. Small coasters used to come in here with cargoes of coal, limestone and other commodities.

The stretch between Bolt Tail and Bolt Head is a fine walk. I did this one April day so hot that I needed several cups of tea on my return to the charming village of Hope. The village, with its many thatched cottages, is tucked into the cliffs at the eastern end of Bigbury Bay. From Bolt Tail across the bay dazzling white shale cliffs shimmered in the strong sunlight. Immediately round Bolt Tail the cliffs rise in spectacular rugged splendour. Near here in 1760 the warship *Ramillies* foundered on rocks during a storm, and 700 sailors lost their lives. Further along some interesting rocks jut out of the cliff top, tor-like, and out to sea stands the Ham Stone. In 1936 the Finnish barque *Herzogen Cecilie* struck the Ham Stone and sank. The coast path then descends to Soar Mill Cove. On a sunny day this is a spot where one wants to linger. There are steep slopes on either side, the eastern rim of shattered angular mica schist being notched like a dragon's back. This stone is used here as a walling material, rather in the manner of the slate in North Wales, being set into the ground end-on in long flat slabs. These weirdly shaped rocks continue past Steeple Cove. At Bolt Head we meet yet another Mew Stone, and across the estuary near Prawle Point is another Ham Stone.

At Start Point Devon turns sharply northwards towards Berry Head and the fleshpots of Torbay. Start Point is perhaps best seen on a stormy day, to extract the most out of the sheer wildness of the place. The lighthouse stands at the end of a serrated ridge of savage rocks that form the spine of the headland. During a winter night here in 1891 five vessels were wrecked in a raging blizzard. From here it is a two mile walk to Hallsands where the haunting remains of a former fishing hamlet stand below the cliffs, at the very edge of a rock shelf. A severe storm on 26 January 1917 engulfed most of the houses. The villagers fled up the cliff and watched as their homes were torn away by the cruel sea, leaving few remains. The disaster had been precipitated by dredging operations in the late nineteenth century, which removed shingle from Start Bay for the construction of Devonport dockyard. This left Hallsands exposed to the ravages of the sea. Amazingly no compensation was paid to the homeless villagers, who had to rely on public donations for support. At one of the ruins waves crashed violently against rocks below the old fireplace with a noise like distant heavy

The Lantern and the Witch
Lantern Rock is a distinctive crag just west of Soar Mill Cove, and as I gazed at it from this angle I could make out a face in the rock to the right. It looked very much like a witch.

David Bellamy

High Peak and Big Picket Rock
Off the red cliffs around Ladram Bay stand a number of isolated rock stacks, some of which look as though they have been gnawed by some enormous sea-squirrel, and left with knobbly bits sticking up at the end.

This painting has been done on De Wint paper, a lovely handmade biscuit-tinted paper that is no longer manufactured. In addition to the normal watercolour palette I have used opaque white gouache to bring out the highlights.

gunfire. I stood there watching the effect of the sea on what was a fairly calm day, pondering on what it must be like in a really rough storm. In the mist the place presented a picture of utter gloom, broken only by the white splashes of a few dog-daisies clinging to the rock. We retired to North Hallsands where there is a superb tea-room that serves the nicest tea-cakes in Devon.

The last time I visited Dartmouth happened to coincide with regatta day, a glorious atmospheric, misty day, although I doubt that many in the crowd would have agreed with that sentiment. The mist was thin enough to enable us to make out the high valley sides in the distance, but strong enough to isolate the ships and vessels, a great help to the artist. This meant less clutter behind the craft, as ancient vessels sailed past the frightfully modern frigate, *HMS Avenger,* her drab grey contrasting with her rows of colourful flags. The town has strong seafaring traditions which can be gauged from the fact that she sent thirty-one ships to the siege of Calais – even more than Plymouth. In 1190 Richard the Lionheart sailed from Dartmouth on his crusade to the Holy Land.

Round Berry Head we come to Torbay, once an important anchorage for the channel fleet during the days of sail, as it was sheltered from the south-westerlies. In January 1866 over ninety sailing vessels had taken refuge here from a fierce southwesterly, when suddenly the wind altered course and began to blow in from the east at hurricane force. The ships were trapped, as it was impossible to sail into a hurricane. One by one their anchor cables snapped and they were quickly smashed to pieces on the rocks by the fury of the waves. Sixty vessels were totally destroyed that night, and next day the shores of Torbay were littered with human and ship debris. Brixham, at the southern end of Torbay, is regarded as the 'Mother of the Trawl Fisheries', for at the end of the eighteenth century its fishermen started using a large mainsail set on a boom and gaff, giving them sufficient power to pull a trawl along the seabed. Before this no fishing boat had been strong enough. From this developed the famous Brixham trawler, which in its heyday was some 300 strong in number. They were extremely robust vessels capable of riding out terrible storms at

Brixham harbour
Brixham was regarded as the 'mother of the trawl fisheries', and though it still has a number of trawlers, it now caters very much for the tourist. My choice of viewpoint here was influenced by the lovely banking of houses above the harbour. Trying to paint each one in would be a nightmare, so I have subdued the upper terraces. In the foreground a channel leads the eye into the harbour itself. Had it not actually been in this position I would probably have moved it slightly to conform with the composition. This painting was done as a demonstration painting for Romsey Art Group.

ABOVE
Exmouth
This is a rough watercolour sketch on cheap cartridge paper. There were many fascinating compositions in this glorious scattering of working boats, and I enjoyed myself immensely sketching, climbing over ropes and getting muddy by wading into positions demanded by the angles of the boats. I never remember to take my wellies!

LEFT
Sidmouth clinker-built tub
These tub-like fishing boats are dragged up the steep shingle beach at Sidmouth by a motor winch.

Seaton Bay

Axmouth harbour by moonlight
Another watercolour carried out on
De Wint paper, which these days I
tend to use as a special treat, dreading
the day it runs out.

sea. It was a Brixham trawler that discovered the rich fishing grounds off the east coast of England, and this heralded the colonization of many east coast ports by Brixham fishermen and their families. With their local fishing grounds declining and so many fishermen working away from home, World War I came as the final straw: not only were many vessels sunk by enemy action, but the sea-bed became littered with many wrecks. These tore the nets to shreds. Trawlers still operate out of the port today, many turning their hand to conveying tourists out on pleasure trips during the summer. With modern radar and charts they are now able to avoid the wrecks. The larger vessels stay out to sea for up to four days at a time. Trawling does devaste the marine life on the sea bottom though, leaving great swathes of sea-desert.

East of Exmouth the long-distance walker following the South Devon coast will find a less complicated route ahead – there are no more wide estuaries to cross. At Exmouth is a delightful jumble of boats, old and new, just waiting for the artist. Beyond the Royal Marines rifle range at Straight Point stands Budleigh Salterton where Sir John Millais used the beach as a setting for his painting *The Boyhood of Raleigh*. At Sidmouth with its steep shingle beach I found the tub-like clinker-built fishing boats made fascinating subjects. These days they are hauled up the beach bow-first by a motor-winch, and launched stern-first. Formerly a large capstan would have been used. When sketching the boats one rainy day I could see the great misty outline of High Peak to the west, with Big Picket Rock jutting up out of the sea below like a rotten tooth. This is perhaps the most interesting section of the coast in East Devon. The cliffs here are rather unstable, and in June 1893 a large piece of High Peak crashed into the sea with a tremendous noise that lasted about ten minutes. It goes without saying that climbing these crumbling cliffs is not recommended. The track along the cliff top to Ladram Bay and beyond gives exhilarating walking, particularly where the towering sea-gnawed red sandstone stacks rise spectacularly out of the water at the bay itself. I did this walk after the countryside had been deluged with several days of heavy rain. As a consequence there were rather a lot of puddles around, and as I jumped over one, my mapcase flew open, disgorging map and several sketches into a muddy puddle. I was not best pleased to find my brand new map and a number of sketches covered in sticky red mud. Unfortunately there is not a single decent mapcase design on the market, which is a shame as they can be so useful for carrying sketches. Behind the coastline stands a huge caravan park, but the beach below hardly seems large enough to cater for everyone. It must be jolly friendly there when the tide is in.

The huge red cliffs of East Devon continue eastwards, punctuated at Branscombe Mouth, Beer and Seaton, but it was the harbour at Axmouth that fascinated me. The combination of water, boats and high cliffs was irresistible. The harbour is actually about a mile from the village, and at its entrance there is an incredibly strong current. Stretching beyond towards Dorset lie the unstable cliffs of the Dowlands Landslip. Here the highly porous topsoil has slipped many times, the most spectacular having occurred on Christmas Eve 1839. Twenty acres of cliff, fields and hedges slid into the sea. Since 1955 it has been a National Nature Reserve.

The waves stretch in sleep,
silvered covers smooth
and tucked in tight-dream-coats
around each bow and stern
of drowsy boats,
their breathing motion slow
and regular –
a rhythmic slap and flow;
unconscious rubbing,
wood on pillow-stones,
like old men scratching,
mumbling, mouths agape,
let soft salt-groans
past harbour lips,
moon-lacquered bright,
and bubbling snores escape
across the bay.

From Axmouth by Moonlight
by Jean M Thomas

Old Harry Rocks
Sketching from a boat in good weather is a pleasant experience, and when there is scenery like this as well, it doubles the pleasure. The view is looking towards Studland Bay.

12
PORTLAND STONE

Bat's Head
At the foot of the great cliff is a small arch
which, with the sea constantly cutting
into it, will gradually become larger.

For much of its length, the Dorset coastline is designated as a Heritage Coast. West Bay, the harbour of Bridport, is, for me, one of the best places in the county to find small working boats to sketch. In the days of sail the harbour had a notorious reputation amongst seafarers. With a narrow sixty-foot wide channel between the wooden piers, plus a wicked sand bar, it is not an easy harbour to enter – or leave, as the sailing vessel *Alioth* found in April 1923. Her German skipper refused a tow by a local boat, and when trying to push the ship away from the piers with boathooks, she ran aground. Despite attempts to refloat her, she eventually broke up during a period of severe gales. West Bay used to be known as Bridport Harbour and was once famous for its nets and rope-making.

Covering a distance of some ten miles west from Portland Bill is Chesil Beach, a seemingly innocuous shingle beach. To sailing ships caught in a south-westerly, however, it was a deadly lee shore. Ships would ground on the steep beach, and any sailor who tried to brave the few feet of waves would be sucked under in no time by the lethal undertow, when just inches from safety. When ships were certain to strike the beach the best action a captain could take was to turn the ship towards the beach and race full tilt in the hope that the momentum would carry the vessel as far up it as possible. In November 1795 six transport ships forming part of a convoy of troopships and merchantmen under Admiral Hugh Christian were wrecked on Chesil during a south-south-westerly gale. No one seems to have found the reason why the pebbles on Chesil Beach are graded in size from the smallest at the west end to the largest near Portland Bill.

For four centuries creamy white Portland Stone has been

LEFT
Durlston Head
This pastel painting shows the view from Winspit at dusk, looking towards Durlston Head with the Anvil Point lighthouse winking in the distance. Below the lighthouse are the Tilly Whim caves, further workings, though not so impressive from the outside as those at Winspit.

RIGHT
Durdle Door
Wide pathways lead to this magnificent arch, giving an idea as to how popular it is with tourists. Whilst I did the original sketch two little tots were playing in the huge surf that crashed onto the beach, swamping them every time.

David Bellamy

quarried on the Isle of Portland and the Isle of Purbeck. The stone is soft enough to carve, and has been used to build St Paul's Cathedral and the United Nations headquarters in New York. These days, of course, much of it goes into cement. On the other side of Portland Bill begins an impressive line of undulating chalk cliffs. After Bat's Head, an impressive sheer chalk buttress, the line of the cliff top drops to the delightfully named Scratchy Bottom. The centre-piece of this striking scenery is Durdle Door, a natural rock arch of Portland stone formed by the action of the sea. It must be one of the most popular attractions on the south coast. Two miles further along is Lulworth Cove, where again the sea has cut into the crumbling chalk cliffs. On a wet summer's day the paths around Lulworth Cove are transformed into long snakes of orange and blue by the mass of tourists in their wet-weather cagoules. Only in few places are paths etched so strikingly into the landscape, the white chalk contrasting with the dark green sward. If you look at the Ordnance Survey map you will see that the area beyond Lulworth Cove runs red with danger signs, signifying an army tank firing range. There is at least one lovely old farm of mellowing Portland stone, slightly overgrown with ivy, the epitome of the English countryside, and in the field in front of it stands a supremely incongruous sign saying 'DANGER UNEXPLODED SHELLS'. The area is rich in wildlife and wild flowers: cowslips, wild parsnip, horseshoe vetch, wild thyme, harebells and milkworts, even wild cabbage. Sea birds and skylarks rub shoulders and there are many varieties of beautiful butterflies. Each year amidst all this beauty some 70,000 rounds of high explosive, armour-piercing and phosphorous shells are fired. Some explode, some don't, and some bounce off things they weren't meant to and end up in places they shouldn't be, so don't touch anything, not even a beer can. You just don't know where it's been. So except at weekends and a period in August and September the coast path is normally closed off.

A mile inland from the sea, surrounded by this no-man's-land, stands the deserted village of Tyneham. Until 1943 this was a peaceful village, but then the army decided to use it as a training ground, promising to give it back when hostilities ended. Over 250 occupants were evacuated from the area. Despite the promises, they were never allowed to return to their homes. The place has an air of ghostly sadness, almost evil, evoking a feeling that the villagers had fled quickly in terror. The exhibition in the village makes great play of how the army have protected the wildlife and rare plants from the ravages of modern Britain. Whilst that is quite true, it is the comments in the visitors' book that speak volumes. Almost all condemn the presence of the military, and question why they continue to remain here, why there is no mention in the exhibition of why it was taken over and the promises made at the time. One entry summed it all up rather well by stating that the exhibition seemed to imply that the army existed solely to preserve the heathland and had nothing to do with warfare and destruction!

I found Chapman's Pool many years ago on a beautiful summer evening when some hippies were camping there, near the old boathouse where lads were fishing. These days the place is considered too dangerous, with the crumbling cliffs, so people are discouraged from going there. Winspit, on the other side of St Alban's Head, is a strange place. The rocks here stand in massive square blocks, piled up in layers to form cliffs; some of them seem about to topple into the sea at the slightest breath of wind. This was one of the large workings where the Purbeck Portland limestone was quarried. Great gaping tunnels run into the cliffs from a ledge above the sea, some held up by pillars left by the quarrymen. In places the fractured rock looked totally unstable. In the inky blackness inside one might expect to find the lair of some quarry demon. Most of the stone was transported in ketches, either lowered over the ledge or put into flat-bottomed rowing boats to be taken out to the waiting ketches. Winspit was a particularly difficult place to load up, and much of the hard won stone ended up at the bottom of the sea. The quarry here was worked well into the twentieth century. An interesting walk of about four miles starts from the pretty village of Worth Matravers, heading directly for the coast at Winspit before turning west along the cliff tops for St Alban's Head. From the coastguard station here a lane leads back to the village.

Further along the coast, near Durlston Head, are more workings at Tilly Whim Caves. 'Whim' comes from the wooden derrick used to lower the stone down to sea-level, and Tilly was the name of the quarry owner. The quarry was worked from around the start of the eighteenth century until 1812. The walk from here to Durlston Head reveals plunging cliff scenery teeming with sea birds. The birds make full use of the massive blocks, some of which look as though they have just fallen into the sea. From the head itself the Isle of Wight is visible some eighteen miles away, with the chalk cliffs culminating in the Needles being prominent. From medieval times Swanage was an important port for the export of Purbeck stone. Then the railway arrived and heralded the death of the port and the birth of tourism. It was in Swanage Bay in 877 that King Alfred gave the Danes a beating.

Geologically the most interesting features of this part of the coastline are the chalk stacks near Studland known as Old Harry Rocks. Some say these were named after Harry Paye, one of the most famous pirates from Poole, whilst others reckon it was after the Devil himself. Argument persists as to whether one of the other stacks is Harry's wife, or whether she took a dive into the sea many years ago. Some have even dared to say that Old Harry is really his wife. Although I have sketched these rocks from the mainland, the most satisfactory composition was gained from out at sea on a boat. The low angle also adds to the drama of the subject, and allows the fascinating caves and arches to be seen to better advantage. On the way out from Swanage other subjects present themselves, and the bird life is far more apparent than it is from the cliffs above. Shags, kittiwakes, fulmars, razorbills and oyster catchers are

Caves at Winspit
These manmade caves were formed when the cliff was quarried for Portland stone, which was in great demand over the centuries. The block-like structure of the rock is quite clear. The foreground is an extensive ledge, from which the stone was lowered onto barges to be taken out to waiting ketches, although on a calm day the ketches would sometimes come in to be loaded directly from above.

The Needles, Isle of Wight
On a clear day the Isle of Wight is plainly visible from Durlston Head, but of course the Needles are then end-on and too far away to see properly. Having whet my appetite on Durlston Head I then shot off to sketch the Needles from broadside on, and was lucky enough to find a lifeboat in the middle distance, struggling through a Force Seven with huge pillars of spray shooting up over it. The Needles are among the best known chunks of rocks to mariners the world over.

just a few of the many birds to be seen along this stretch. Provided the sea is reasonably calm, sketching from a boat can be great fun, and offers a totally new perspective – also there is physically little effort involved. Unless you are rowing, of course. Having done it many times, I do recommend trying to sketch from a boat, but if, like me, you get lost in your work, make sure someone is with you to keep an eye on where you may be drifting! Our trip to Old Harry passed without incident, apart from Popple almost falling overboard. For the uninitiated a Popple is a sort of purple teddy-bear with a long tail, which can retreat mysteriously into its own fur coat. Catherine always seems to have hers with her on holiday!

13
PAINTING THE COAST

Galway hooker *Mac Duach*
Tied up against Kinvara Quay this
beautiful old hooker made a superb
subject. When painting a boat I try
to capture the essential
characteristics of the vessel, and here
it was the sharply raked stern and
graceful lines. Hookers have a
bulbous type of hull which is best
seen end-on, but in this view the
sunlight caught the bulge just
forward of midships where I have
indicated with the light patch. These
vessels were used to carry turf out to
the Aran Isles, and many can still be
seen around Galway. A smaller
version, called a *gleoiteog* pronounced
'glowchug', is also fairly common.

In this chapter I shall outline some of the methods I use for sketching on location and working up paintings at home. Emphasis will be placed on those aspects of coastal and marine painting that amateur artists find challenging. In particular I shall be discussing waves, boats, rocks, and working on the coast. For those who wish to know more about my working methods I would refer them to my previous book *Painting in the Wild*, which is a comprehensive guide to painting in watercolour. I also hope that many non-painters will find this chapter of interest, in seeing how the final painting evolves from being just an impression in the mind of the artist.

Nearly all my painting is done from sketches carried out in front of the subject: only very occasionally do I do a full painting outside. This approach has several advantages: firstly it means I can keep my equipment to a minimum; secondly I'm not afraid to make a mess by working quickly or in bad conditions; and thirdly I can re-state the composition, if necessary,

back in the studio. Against this is the argument that a certain amount of spontaneity is lost when working indoors. Anyway, what suits me may well not suit every artist, so really it is a good idea to try each method and see which one suits you best. Working my way also has the advantage that one is less conspicuous when people are around, and the work done outdoors can be kept as a permanent reference.

My sketching equipment is kept as simple as possible. Unless working near the car I normally carry everything in a rucksack. This leaves my arms free for clambering over rocks, down harbour ladders and when walking along. It is also far less tiring. A small daysack can be bought cheaply in mountain gear shops, preferably with at least one external pocket, so that you can keep brushes, pencils, paints, palette and small sketchbook together and easily accessible. Larger sketchbooks can be kept inside, in a polythene bag, as no rucksack is completely waterproof. My pencils and brushes are stored in a strong

Beach at Newgale
Only Payne's Grey was used in this watercolour sketch. Doing a monochrome in this way is excellent practice as the artist can forget about colours and concentrate on tone, which really is more important even than colour in most landscapes.

plastic tube. The palette I prefer for outdoor work is a small aluminium one manufactured by Daler-Rowney, as it does not break. I carry loose cartridge and watercolour papers in a mapcase with more inside the rucksack, in addition to sketchbooks. The Daler-Rowney spiral-bound A5 books are convenient for rapid sketching, as they fit so easily into a pocket. A larger one is kept in the rucksack, and this acts as a firm support as well. I prefer to use tubes of watercolour paint, as large amounts can be squeezed out if needed. The main colours that I use are as follows:

Raw Sienna	French Ultramarine	Raw Umber
Cobalt Blue	Crimson Alizarin	Payne's Grey
Burnt Sienna	Cadmium Yellow Light	Lemon Yellow
Burnt Umber	Cadmium Red	Light Red

As well as ordinary pencils I take a selection of watercolour pencils. I do not carry an easel around as I like to be very mobile: scrambling around on cliffs and rocks with an easel could be really awkward, and it would be likely to jam in some crevices. For a seat I use a Karrimat, available from mountain gear shops. It is a closed-cell foam pad nearly half an inch (nine millimetres) thick which will protect you from mud, snow or sharp rocks. It can be cut to any size you wish, weighs very little and will bend easily to fit your bag or rucksack.

To get the most out of a day's sketching on the coast it is as well to have an idea as to when high tide will occur, what the main features of the part of the coast you wish to explore are, and what routes to take. Ideally I like to leave the car and spend the whole day walking and sketching, perhaps taking in one or two harbours in the walk. In some harbours it is easy to park, others it is not. For example, Looe or Polperro in summer are extremely difficult, so in that instance I would drive to Talland Bay and walk east or west along the coast to whichever place I

Approaching storm, River Orwell
Normally Pin Mill is a placid place, and on this afternoon my friend Eric and I strolled in the sunshine admiring the old barges before I settled down to sketch. Then, with a bang, the storm arrived, and this watercolour sketch shows the scene just before it reached the Orwell. The barge has been finished in haste so that I could get it under cover. Eric ran into the trees and I took up a new position to sketch in 'storm mode'. Soon everything was dripping wet, sketch and artist.

LEFT
Storm on the River Orwell
This watercolour shows the same scene as the sketch, only the storm has now arrived! It was preceded by a fierce wind and continued monsoon-like, with rain hammering down nonstop and lightning flashing without pause. I was so taken with it that I even forgot to put a coat on. Suffolk may not be a terribly wild coast, but it certainly has some wild moments. These barges are popular subjects for artists, and sixteen of them even took part in the evacuation of Dunkirk in 1940. It must have been a stirring sight for the British Tommies on the Dunkirk beaches to see the red sails of these magnificent vessels approaching.

RIGHT
Boat at Fishguard
By making the boat small relative to the overall size of the painting, I have accentuated the feeling of loneliness. The lighting is coming from almost directly above, perhaps a more unusual treatment. Consideration of the direction of the lighting is vital before putting brush to paper.

wanted to visit, taking in the coastline one way and perhaps returning by an inland route. Getting there early also helps. Even on a Bank Holiday places like Clovelly in North Devon are still fairly sleepy first thing in the morning. If you are particularly interested in boats and ships then obviously visiting a place when the local regatta is on will yield dividends. Events such as the sailing barge matches in East Anglia and the Medway, the Tall Ships Race, the East Coast Old Gaffers Race and the *Cruinniú na mbad* at Kinvara in Galway Bay will give many hours of sketching these lovely sailing vessels.

Painting by the sea poses a number of new problems not associated with landscape painting. The sea is ever-moving, even at its calmest, and does not stand still whilst you paint each detail. The tide changes the angle that boats lie at their moorings. The bare rock and cliffs displaying prominent strata lines, and a variety of colours, can be deceptively difficult to the unwary. I shall cover all these aspects shortly, but first would like to say a few words on composition. Many artists make life difficult for themselves by selecting an awkward viewpoint, without exploring the possibilities. It is all too easy to walk along the cliff tops, see a view and start painting, without trying to improve the composition by getting down to shore-level, for example. Obviously there are times when it would be suicidal to climb down the cliffs, but if it is safe to do so, I often find the lower viewpoint much easier from the perspective aspect, and also it adds a certain amount of drama. If possible I almost get down into the water to get a 'flotsam' viewpoint. Move about until you are happy with the angle of view, but

Cliffs of Moher
A sheer drop of about 700 feet (214 metres) takes your breath away on the top of these cliffs in Co Clare. Here I have used the watersoluble graphite pencil with a wet brush, trying not to put too much detail on the cliff face as it was in direct sunlight. To give the impression of sunlight put in as little detail as you can get away with.

bear in mind that if the tide is coming in you may have to move quickly, either to avoid being stranded, or being forced to take a new viewpoint. Use foreground rocks, boats, lobster pots, bits of seaweed, and so on to lead you into the picture, or to frame the centre of interest. Try to pick out a strong centre of interest, or accentuate one that is not too prominent; it helps not to have more than one such point.

Much of the time when sketching I like to use watercolour. Quite often it hardly takes any longer than a pencil sketch, and of course if I want to capture atmosphere and colour it is unrivalled. If the subject is complicated I begin with an ordinary pencil drawing, then use colour when the first stage is complete. Most of the time though I prefer a combination of watercolour and watercolour pencil, by first laying on the main washes of watercolour and then working into the wet washes with the watercolour pencils. Generally I only use the dark colours for this, although I have done many sketches using several coloured pencils. Watercolour pencils are a superb and very much underrated sketching medium. The Derwent ones by Rexel are superb for creating a whole range of colours, as they seem to blend better than others on the market. Used on their own, or with pure watercolour washes, they will happily work away whilst the rain is pouring down: you don't have to stop for the torrential downpour or to let things dry! Some subjects of course can be covered rapidly and without fuss simply by using an ordinary pencil, writing in colour notes if needed. I also like the Derwent Drawing pencils which have a waxy composition and come in a number of subtle colours:

Thumbnail sketch for Kinlochbervie
On a complicated painting I often do a number of these small thumbnail sketches in monochrome, three or four inches long. This was the composition chosen for the Kinlochbervie painting.

Chocolate, Brown Ochre, Terracotta, Venetian Red, as well as Ivory Black. A more recent development is the watersoluble graphite pencil manufactured by Rexel and Berol in a few degrees of softness. These can be used like ordinary pencils, but by floating water over them lovely washes of soft tones can be produced. They are extremely useful when quick, simple sketches are needed where a tone or atmosphere is important, and there are many examples in this book.

Observation is the key to successful sketching, and this is true of all elements within the composition: colour, tone, shape, perspective, recession. As artists we should have no pre-conception of what things look like, and I might even go so far as to say, in certain circumstances, 'don't use your brains – rely on your eyes!' This I find is at its most obvious when students are painting distant wooded hills in summer. All too frequently the hills are painted in the same colour and tone of green that is used on foreground foliage, without taking into account the effect of the atmosphere. Only by deliberately comparing the foreground greens with the far distant greens can you see the difference. This question of comparison should be constantly uppermost in the mind of the artist. Compare colours, tones, sizes, angles and just about everything, to see how each element

ABOVE
Paglesham
Again it was Eric who dragged me (not unwillingly) to the ends of Essex where we found this tranquil scene. The rotting carcass of an old boat is still securely moored, despite being firmly embedded in several feet of Essex mud! In the treatment of figures I like to cut them off just below the knee, and not include the feet. Somehow this makes people resemble a Walt Disney character, like Goofy for example. Figures, I feel, are essential in a harbour scene, to avoid the ghost-town impression.

RIGHT
Kinlochbervie at night
Sketching in a harbour at night is not too difficult, and does make a change from normal work. It was really the effects of the lights that fascinated me, and how they picked out detail on the boats moored at the quay. Only a suggestion of the buildings has been put in.

of the composition relates to its neighbour. Sometimes it is handy to have a pair of binoculars available, not so much to actually work from, but to help gain a better understanding of distant parts of a subject. An example of this might be the detail in a complicated boat, where the artist might wish to work out exactly where some of the ropes end up. Try to keep the composition as simple and uncluttered as possible.

Back in the studio I produce final paintings from the sketches, using photographs to back them up. Sometimes I use two or three sketches as a basis for the painting, depending on the size and complexity. Photographs can be helpful to check angles, detail and the sizes of the various elements, and I find them particularly useful in crowded harbours where there is often the problem of which mast and rigging belongs to which boat. Taking a series of photographs from different positions can help to identify such detail. Of course, nothing beats doing a number of sketches if you can. In many cases I do two or three little thumbnail sketches in monochrome, based on the original sketch, to help decide on the final composition. Normally I use pencils, but the graphite watersoluble pencils are superb for this if you need to include tone on the thumbnail sketch. Such sketches can help you decide, for example, how many boats to put in, how high to put the horizon line, or whether to include that extra group of rocks. It is at this stage that I decide on the atmosphere and whether any emphasis needs changing within the composition, all the time being careful to retain the character of the location. I mainly paint in watercolour, and do not use watercolour pencils or really anything other than traditional watercolour techniques for the final painting. Pastel is another medium I enjoy using now and then, and occasionally I carry out an oil painting. Switching to another medium is an excellent way to get out of the rut we artists find ourselves in from time to time. Most of the watercolours reproduced in this book were painted on Saunders Waterford 140 lb paper, although I do use Arches paper from time to time. With watercolour paper it is always best to try out what is on the market before settling down to use one particular brand.

With marine or coastal painting there are a few aspects that tend to put off some artists who feel quite at ease with landscape work. Water is perhaps the chief concern, and in particular waves. Cameras tend to freeze the action of waves and potentially lead us to produce work which lacks any feeling of movement. Perhaps video cameras are an improvement, but not everyone wants to carry all the equipment around with them! Like anything else, you really have to observe the action of the waves critically. Sit there for a while absorbing the movements. Watch how the waves break, then tumble in a mass of seething foam and expend themselves on the beach. Note also how they break furiously onto rocks, followed by little cascades of white water as it falls back into the sea. The large waves that catch the eye don't appear one after another non-stop. There will be a break when smaller waves come in, so it needs patience to watch for these big waves, observe how they break and fall, and then get it down on paper immediately. Sometimes it is a good idea to use a reasonably large piece of paper and do two little sketches on it at the same time. In this way you can sketch the wave as it arrives, then do a study of rocks, perhaps, whilst waiting for the next wave. Note where the light catches the water as it tumbles. There is no easy formula for painting waves: it is really a case of getting out there and studying them carefully.

Boats and ships are perhaps among the most beautiful things that man has designed, but tend to be notoriously difficult to paint, unless seen from directly abeam. Some tutors recommend drawing a construction box with a figure eight at the top to help get the curves right. Personally I've never used this method, and I feel that it detracts from a watercolour painting in particular, as one has to get rid of construction lines. This inevitably means a loss of freshness about the final work. Here again, observation and practice is the key. Take extra care when plotting the critical points on the boat, that is, the extremities and where the bowline and sternline meet the water or ground. Sometimes it may help to mark these positions with a dot before committing yourself. If the boat is lying on its side it becomes an even greater challenge. In this case I find it useful sometimes to determine the line of the vertical and work from there. Obviously if the craft has a mast this is no problem,

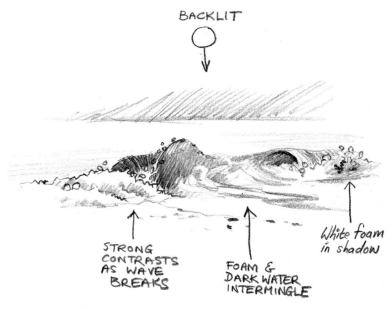

Drawing a wave
A This is a photograph of a wave breaking near the beach, showing the water curving over to spill as a mass of foam.

B In this simplified diagram the wave shown in the photograph is analyzed.

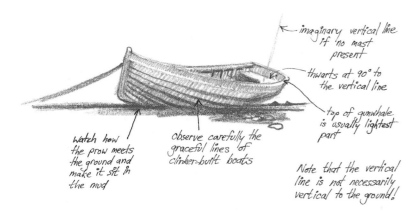

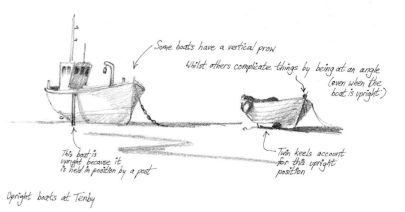

Drawing boats
Drawings of boats to illustrate ways of tackling the problem.

Old harbour, Newlyn
This is a quiet backwater of Newlyn, with lovely old stonework on the quay and slip. In this watercolour I have subdued the background houses so as to encourage the viewer to concentrate on the harbour.

Stiffkey Salt Marshes, Norfolk
Stiffkey Marshes on a misty day make a strange landscape where it is easy to become disorientated. In places it is very muddy, and there are many wooden bridges, several of which are redundant because of silting up. As I sat in the mud sketching, several locals walked past to gather cockles, their gabbled conversation coming to a sudden halt when they caught sight of me. Once past they began chatting away again in earnest. In places it was impossible to determine where sky met land or water, and my watercolours quickly became spattered with sand. I chose Derwent pastels for this final painting.

and some craft are easier than others. The line of the rudder or centre-line of a cabin can sometimes give an idea where the vertical comes. Once the vertical has been established the horizontal lines across stern, cabin and thwarts can be drawn – if in fact all these apply. Then the remaining lines can be entered using the first ones as a guide. This is not foolproof, but it does offer a start. Beware sketching boats in one location, or at one state of the tide, and then fitting them into a painting of a different location or time, as the perspective can vary considerably. This is where thumbnail sketches will help you decide if the perspective is uniform. When sketching keep an eye on the tide as it can quickly change the angle of the boat. Undoubtedly the quickest way to learn to draw boats is to practise, practise, and eventually those lovely curves will fall off the tip of your pencil.

Many students have problems with rocks. There are so many different kinds of rock it really does pay to observe carefully what is in front of you and try to capture the character of the rock. This is betrayed by the colour, shape, and type of fractures. In places on the coast you will find a great many colours in the rock. In the small cove of Porthselau near St David's, for example, there is almost every colour imaginable in the rock face. Naturally, in such a situation it would be best to simplify the amount of colours, and in most cases, unless there was a hard transition, blend them gradually into one another. This softness should contrast with the sharp edges of the rock itself, as well as the cracks and fissures which help to give it character. Try to avoid painting them in at one per inch (two centimetres) like a line of emaciated worms climbing up the face. Give them character by watching how they begin, how wide they become, and how they end. Are they basically horizontal, vertical or angled? Are they contorted into some strange pattern? Note also how the light strikes them, usually making the horizontal surfaces much lighter than the others. Then, once you are adept at painting rocks you can begin losing them in the spray and mist of wild waves, changing nature to suit your needs. As the Neo-Classicist Valenciennes wrote 'Happy is the artist who lets himself be swayed by the delights of illusion and so imagines he sees nature as it ought to be.' In the main your work is bound to improve by practising on marine subjects regularly, by careful observation, and by not trying anything too ambitious until you are ready.

Boats at Blakeney, Norfolk
Old salts seem to be much fewer on the ground these days, so I try to sketch them whenever I get the opportunity. The figures shown here are all of the same person. Sometimes I work on two or even three drawings at once if the person is moving around.

14
WALKING THE COAST

Carnllidi
This is viewed from Porthselau, near St David's. The ruggedness of Carnllidi deceives the eye, for it is less than 600 feet (181 metres) high. A marvellous circular walk can be done around St David's Head taking in Caerfai Bay, Ramsey Sound, Whitesand Bay and the head itself, or for the more ambitious from Solva right round to Abereiddi. It is truly one of the best coastal walks in the country, with interest throughout for artist and nature-lover alike. This is a quick watercolour sketch done on cartridge paper.

The joys of coastal walking, whether along the cliff top, beach or harbour wall, give endless pleasure and rewards to those who make the effort, even in poor weather. Apart from the magnetic appeal of the sea, with the ebb and flow of the tides, there always seems to be something of interest happening along the shore: the wildlife in the rock pools, in the air, or on the cliffs; the action of the waves; the rock formations, caves, arches and pinnacles; the fishermen with their boats, their lobster pots, nets and buoys. The list is endless. Walking the coast is now an extremely popular activity, whether along one of the official long-distance paths, a Heritage Coast, or simply just where there is a path. Some do it for exercise, some for the beauty, some to walk their dogs, some even to paint the scenery, and maybe there are one or two who still do it to elude the Revenue men. Whatever the reason, in this chapter I shall endeavour to pass on some of my experiences on the practicalities of walking by the sea.

It goes without saying that the coast is a pretty dangerous place. People get cut off by the tide, fall off cliffs, overturn boats, knock themselves out wind-surfing, slip on rocks, get dragged under by undertows and washed out to sea by strong currents. If you do see someone in difficulties, ring the coastguard straight away, whether it's red flares, people in the sea or a man in a dinghy waving his trousers aloft. Tide tables can usually be obtained locally from harbour towns, tourist information centres and sometimes local newspapers. There is normally some six hours thirteen minutes between high and low tide, and high tide is usually about fifty minutes later on each successive day. The unwary can easily be cut off by the tide as it does not come in at a constant pace. From low tide: during the first hour it will come in at one-twelfth, the second hour at twice this speed, and the third and fourth hours each at three-twelfths, with the fifth and sixth hours slowing down to two-twelfths and one-twelfth respectively. Currents are usually at their strongest off headlands and between islands, as at Ramsey Sound in Pembrokeshire where the current looks fearsome if you stand on the mainland opposite the Bitches. Weather forecasts are now available on the telephone via Marinecall. If you do need advice don't hesitate to ring the coastguard, especially if you intend doing something potentially dangerous. The coastguards are very approachable and only too glad to help, but if you tell them you're doing a channel crossing in a bath-tub, do let them know when you return, so that the helicopters, long-range search aircraft, lifeboats, coastguard rescue companies, and probably men in white coats, are not all out looking for your bath-tub.

For the walker the main problems are slippery paths, crumbling cliff edges, and perhaps wading across estuaries. Erosion is naturally taking place all the time and you have only to spend a few days along the coast to see examples of fairly recent rock falls. In places it is happening regularly, as some cliffs are more susceptible than others to crumbling. Beware particularly of cliffs which at the start of a walk appear firm, only to change without warning where one type of rock abuts another, and the cliff becomes a mixture of earth and pebbles, and totally unsafe. Don't expect the coastal authorities to label every hazard clearly: it would be an impossible task for them. Sadly, in these days when many of our cities are sprouting railings everywhere, funnelling everyone as though into a trawler-net, we are perhaps as a consequence made oblivious to danger when confronted with it on a cliff top.

Apart from studying the guidebooks, take local advice if you are in doubt about anything. Some estuaries can be crossed safely at low tide, but don't just assume it – find out. Some rocks are more slippery than others, and many are lethal whatever the weather, and here trainers are totally inadequate footwear. Although light and comfortable, ordinary trainers can be a killer even on dry rock. I once walked a short way along the shore from Abercastle in Pembrokeshire in completely dry conditions in trainers. Suddenly my legs shot from under me and my left hand smashed against a rock, the full force being taken by my Sony portable tape recorder. Amazingly I recovered without falling and despite a dent the recorder went on happily working. I take my hat off to Sony, as reliability these days is a very precious attribute. For my main walking I wear Scarpa boots which give an extremely firm grip in all conditions, and have proved unbeatable. Boots are the most important piece of equipment for coastal walking, so it's sensible to

Loch Duich, Western Highlands
At the head of this great sea-loch are the Five Sisters of Kintail, at their most impressive under winter conditions. Apart from the mountains there are many opportunities for walking round the shores of these sea-lochs. The western side of Loch Duich is the more interesting walk, with its superb views, and away from the main road.

get the best you can. Waterproofs come in all shapes and sizes, but I found that when I switched to using the Gore-tex *Alpine Extrem* jacket by Berghaus the breathable fibre made hard walking infinitely more comfortable in bad weather.

Although I camp wild in the mountains, I only do so as a last resort on the coast. This is mainly because being so close to population centres the water is suspect. Many of the coastal areas have the worst water pollution in the country, with some of the water authorities themselves as the worst offenders. This does not bode well for the coastal backpacker, not to mention the holidaymaker and those living in the area. There are however many campsites, ranging from good to abysmal. At one Cornish site I sat eating the evening meal watching a young couple spend well over an hour erecting a tent. After twenty minutes or so, in a state of half-erection, it wobbled alarmingly, rather like two back ends of a pantomime horse trying to escape, before the inevitable collapse.

On another occasion, however, the laugh was on me. After a tiring fifteen-mile walk, on seeing a campsite from the cliff top, I asked a chap the quickest way through the maze of streets. At his suggestion I walked to the top of the street, through a gate and up the field next to the site. At this point his 'just a hop over the fence' went sadly awry. What confronted me resembled the Maginot Line: barbed wire, high fence, rocks, dense undergrowth and a steep bank. For all I knew there may well have been an anti-tank ditch on the other side. Against my better judgement I decided to tackle it. Flinging my fibre-pile jacket over the barbed wire, I scrambled up a large square boulder, gasping at the weight of my huge backpack, and fending off more barbed wire at the same time. I then hacked my way through dense undergrowth to reach the fourth obstacle, a high bank covered with massed nettles. Again the jacket came in handy to smother the nettles, and the only resort with any strays was to head-butt them out of the way. Then, with a

OPPOSITE
Walberswick
This lovely old Suffolk village with its rickety old shanties has provided me with many happy hours of sketching. The walk to Southwold is a pleasant stroll, using the ferry just upriver from this point. On an ebb tide the ferryman has quite a job to row across. He rows upriver in quieter water then virtually lets the boat drift across in the strong current. With a full load it can't be easy and I saw him once with several large ladies, the boat almost shipping water, so low was his freeboard.

LEFT
Polperro
A monochrome watercolour sketch.

High Sharpnose Point
Jagged cliffs thrust out into the Atlantic along this stretch of the Cornish coast, making it a visual delight for walker, artist and those who love wild romantic places. Many a ship foundered below these cliffs. Care is needed as the drops are particularly severe.

Carn Lês Boel
Walking south easterly from Land's End a number of spectacular granite headlands are encountered, and Carn Lês Boel, with its amazing pinnacles, is probably the most impressive of all.

great heave I joyfully emerged out of the undergrowth onto the top of the bank like some earth-bound Neptune, much to the consternation of those in the nearest caravan. I didn't dare look at them, just grinned broadly to display a hint of friendliness, as by now I looked like a vegetated rustic sprouting all sorts of hedgerow vegetation. Gingerly I stepped out onto a bush, hoping it would hold my weight. Barbed wire was strung neck-high below me, with a gap between bush and wire. I poised ready to jump, mindful of the need to clear the wire, then flew through the air with the elegance of a flying octopus, landing with a deafening crash. From the caravan I could hear cups being dropped as everyone rushed to one side to see where the rustic flying Neptune had landed. I gathered myself together, tried to remove as much vegetation as possible, brushed myself down and set off for the Reception, unaware that a nettle stuck prominently out of my hair. Needless to say, I was relieved to get into the tent. My tent is a Peapod by Ultimate Equipment. It is light and has even survived the odd hurricane without mishap. For years I carried my backpacking gear around in a battered old rucksack that produced red-raw weals on my back after a number of days in the wilds. Switching to a modern

sack, the Berghaus Scorpion, has made a world of difference to the comfort and state of my back, and is easy to use.

In addition to the official long-distance paths of the coastal section of the Cleveland Way, the Pembrokeshire Coast Path and the South-West Way from Minehead in Somerset to Poole in Dorset, there are a great many walking opportunities amongst the Heritage Coasts where many footpaths are being restored. Perhaps I am putting my head on the block by mentioning some of my favourites, but those that spring to mind are the Hartland Point stretch in North Devon, north from Bude in Cornwall, the southern coast of the Land's End peninsula, the Gower coast from Port Eynon to Worms Head and most of the Pembrokeshire Coast Path. But half the fun is in finding those lovely deserted coves and creeks away from the main routes. Despite the calculated indifference of those in authority, there are many organizations actively striving for the preservation of the British coast. Sadly, much of the damage has already been done, but there is still a tremendous amount of beauty out there to be enjoyed. We must ensure, for the sake of our children, and future generations, that it remains a place of supreme wild enchantment.

Penberth
Cornwall is full of delightful narrow coves into which they've somehow managed to cram a hamlet or even village. Penberth is a gem of a cove, and because few cars can get there there were few people around as I sketched in the sunshine.

The Knave, Gower
Here the angled structure of the limestone cliffs is distinct, and gives an indication of the severe switchback nature of the terrain that walkers have to cover if they wish to keep reasonably close to the sea. Believe me, it's pretty tiring, but the visual impact of such scenery over-compensates for any blisters or aches! I have not exaggerated the feature in any way – honest!

Lydstep Point, Pembrokeshire

Although I have been here many times, it was a wild day in August when rain lashed down, the wind howled across the sea and huge breakers crashed against the rocky bastions below. Caldey Island was just about visible to the right. I sat huddled in the deluge enjoying every minute, even though in the roar of sea and wind I could not hear myself sing – perhaps it's just as well: I'm a terrible singer.

Sea-painter and poet, a weaver of dreams,
elemental translator of abstract extremes,
designer, creator, green-demons of art
whip storm-inspirations to salt-lash my heart.

The painter is watching; the poet he hears
the song of the humpback, the wave-dragon rears
and roars of the fate of the philistine man
sucked back to the dark where the circle began.

Jean M Thomas

SELECT BIBLIOGRAPHY

AA, *Illustrated Guide to Britain's Coast*, (AA Publications, 1987)

Barrett, John H, *The Pembrokeshire Coast Path*, (HMSO, 1974)

Bellamy, David, *Painting in the Wild*, (Webb & Bower, 1988)

Edmunds, George, *The Gower Coast*, (Regional Publications, 1986)

Falconer, Alan, *The Cleveland Way*, (HMSO, 1972)

Gant, Roland, *A Guide to the South Devon & Dorset Coast Paths*, (Constable, 1982)

Goddard, Ted, *Pembrokeshire Shipwrecks*, (Christopher Davies, 1988)

Greenpeace, *Coastline*, (Kingfisher Books, 1987)

Gunnell, Clive, *Somerset & North Devon Coast Path*, (HMSO, 1981)

Hughes, Emrys, & Aled Eames, *Porthmadog Ships*, (Gwynedd Archives Service, 1975)

John, Brian, *Pembrokeshire*, (Greencroft Books, 1976)

Le Messurier, Brian, *South Devon Coast Path*, (HMSO, 1980)

Ortzen, Len, *Famous Lifeboat Rescues*, (Arthur Barker, 1971)

Pyatt, Edward C, *Cornwall Coast Path*, (HMSO, 1976)

Seymour, John, *The Companion Guide to the Coast of South-West England*, (Collins, 1974)

Skidmore, Ian, *Anglesey & Lleyn Shipwrecks*, (Christopher Davies, 1979)

Traditional Sail Review is a magazine available from 28, Spital Road, Maldon, Essex CM9 6EB, and is a mine of information about events in the traditional sailing boat calendar.

INDEX

Italics refer to page showing illustration